Roller Coasters

TECHNOLOGY 360

Roller Coasters

Jenny MacKay

LUCENT BOOKS
A part of Gale, Cengage Learning

Detroit • New York • San Francisco • New Haven, Conn • Waterville, Maine • London

LIBRARY OF CONGRESS CATALOGING-IN-PUBLICATION DATA

MacKay, Jenny, 1978-
    Roller coasters / by Jenny MacKay.
        p. cm. – (Technology 360)
    Includes bibliographical references and index.
    ISBN 978-1-4205-0825-3 (hbk.)
  1. Roller coasters—Juvenile literature. 2. Roller coasters—Design and construction—Juvenile literature. I. Title.
    GV1860.R64M34 2013
    791.068--dc23
    2012021423

Lucent Books
27500 Drake Rd
Farmington Hills MI 48331

ISBN-13: 978-1-4205-0825-3
ISBN-10: 1-4205-0825-3

Printed in the United States of America
1 2 3 4 5 6 7 16 15 14 13 12

CONTENTS

FOREWORD

"As we go forward, I hope we're going to continue to use technology to make really big differences in how people live and work."
—Sergey Brin, co-founder of Google

The past few decades have seen some amazing advances in technology. Many of these changes have had a direct and measureable impact on the way people live, work, and play. Communication tools, such as cell phones, satellites, and the Internet, allow people to keep in constant contact across longer distances and from the most remote places. In fields related to medicine, existing technologies—digital imaging devices, robotics and lasers, for example—are being used to redefine surgical procedures and diagnostic techniques. As technology has become more complex, however, so have the related ethical, legal, and safety issues.

Psychologist B.F. Skinner once noted that "the real problem is not whether machines think but whether men do." Recent advances in technology have, in many cases, drastically changed the way people view the world around them. They can have a conversation with someone across the globe at lightning speed, access a huge universe of information with the click of a key, or become an avatar in a virtual world of their own making. While advances like these have been viewed as a great boon in some quarters, they have also opened the door to questions about whether or not the speed of technological advancement has come at an unspoken price. A closer examination of the evolution and use of these devices provides a deeper understanding of the social, cultural and ethical implications that they may hold for our future.

Technology 360 not only explores how evolving technologies work, but also examines the short- and long-term impact of their use on society as a whole. Each volume in Technology 360 focuses on a particular invention, device or family of similar devices, exploring how the device was developed; how it works; its impact on society; and possible future uses. Volumes also contain a chronology specific to each topic, a glossary of technical terms used in the text, and a subject index. Sidebars, photos and detailed illustrations, tables, charts and graphs help further illuminate the text.

Titles in this series emphasize inventions and devices familiar to most readers, such as robotics, digital cameras, iPods, and video games. Not only will users get an easy-to-understand, "nuts and bolts" overview of these inventions, they will also learn just how much these devices have evolved. For example, in 1973 a Motorola cell phone weighed about two pounds and cost $4000.00—today, cell phones weigh only a few ounces and are inexpensive enough for every member of the family to have one. Lasers—long a staple of the industrial world—have become highly effective surgical tools, capable of reshaping the cornea of the eye and cleaning clogged arteries. Early video games were played on large machines in arcades; now, many families play games on sophisticated home systems that allow for multiple players and cross-location networking.

IMPORTANT DATES

1600s

Russian ice slides, the first-known gravity rides, become popular

1959

Disneyland's Matterhorn Bobsleds becomes world's first tubular steel-track coaster

1874

Pennsylvania's Mauch Chunk Railway is repurposed into a ride for tourists

1927

Cyclone roller coaster opens at Coney Island, New York

1817

First wheeled coaster rides operate in France

1902

Leap-the-Dips becomes first coaster with wheels that grip the outer edges of the track

1907

Lap-bar restraint used for the first time in a coaster

1800

1900

1950

1884

Switchback Railway ride opens at Coney Island, New York

Opening of the first roller coaster to operate in a circuit and end where it begins

1885

First chain-operated lift hill used in a roller coaster

1953

Japan's first major roller coaster opens

in the Development of Roller Coasters

1976
Revolution opens in California with the first full loop inversion in a modern roller coaster, using an ovular instead of circular shape

1981
World's first suspended coaster, the Bat, opens in Ohio

1982
World's first stand-up coaster opens in Japan

2001
X opens in California, the first 4th dimension ride featuring independently swiveling seats

1996
First coasters to use magnetic propulsion (linear induction motors) as a launch system open in Ohio and Virginia

2010
Formula Rossa opens at Ferrari World in Abu Dhabi, United Arab Emirates, using a hydraulic launch system to set a new coaster-speed record of 149 mph (240kmph)

1980

2000

2020

2000
Ohio's Millennium Force, the world's first gigacoaster, sets new record for tallest and fastest roller coaster drop

2005
Kingda Ka in New Jersey becomes the world's tallest coaster at 456 ft (139m)

2000
Son of Beast in Ohio becomes first wooden coaster with a full-inversion loop

2011
Takabisha at Fuji-Q Highland in Japan sets a new world record for the steepest vertical coaster drop, 121 degrees

An Industry Built on Adrenaline

I n May 2012, crowds of people in Toronto, Canada, lined up to get a close look at Leviathan for the first time. Named after a colossal and deadly sea serpent rearing its hungry head from the ocean depths of ancient myth, the Leviathan at the Wonderland theme park is a twisted concoction of ocean-blue steel track stretching more than a mile (1.6km) long. It plummets trains of cars over mammoth rises and twists them through loops as though they are on the back of the very beast that gave the ride its name. Passengers riding the Leviathan ascend a 306-foot (93m) rise, one of the tallest lift hills in the world, before losing their breath during an almost vertical descent at a speed of 92 miles per hour (148kph). It takes three minutes and twenty-eight seconds to conquer the beast by reaching its tail end.

Although the visitors to Wonderland, who arrive in the parking lot to see the monster's back curving ominously over the entrance gates, expect to be scared by the thrilling ride, they know Leviathan is not actually dangerous. It is merely one of the newest members of a worldwide family fledged in steel and twenty-eight hundred members strong, all sharing the business of giving riders a few gut-wrenching moments of thrills without putting them in any real peril. Leviathan

is among the largest, fastest, and scariest of its kind, but it belongs to a common breed of machines built the world over for the sole purpose of fun—the roller coaster.

The era of the roller coaster began in the United States at least as early as the 1800s during a period of stark ingenuity and daring innovation. It spawned a surging new fad of thrill rides. Amusement parks today are found on every continent but Antarctica, and coasters are most parks' biggest attractions. Like most technological inventions that got their start more than a century ago, roller coasters have changed in shape, form, and structure, but they have also retained many of the basic design principles that have made them so much fun from the beginning. The same simple rules of physics that spawned early roller coaster models can still be seen at work in Leviathan and its contemporary peers in the United States and around the world, and the terrifying sensations thrill seekers have coveted through history are amplified and perfected in modern coasters.

The roller coaster Leviathan looms over the Wonderland amusement park in Toronto, Canada. It's one of the largest and fastest roller coasters in the world.

CHAPTER 1

Thrill Rides, Then and Now

Entertainment, profit, and the peculiar engineering challenge of designing a ride that is utterly terrifying yet perfectly safe have been the main forces driving the development of roller coasters for the past two hundred years. The popularity of these mechanical marvels has fluctuated over the years, but through the thrill-ride industry's booms and busts, coaster designers and engineers have pursued an ongoing quest to build bigger, better, faster machines that create ever more dramatic thrills for their riders.

Early Coasters

Many modern roller coasters are giant, twisting, snakelike contraptions, and as complex as these rides have become, each owes its existence to all the thrill rides that have come before. Today's roller coasters, many of them grand in size and baffling in their complexity, have evolved from thousands of simpler models created over the years. Some of those models have been more successful than others, but designers have learned from all of them. No modern coaster would exist today if past generations had not thought to create the first thrill rides. The roller coaster's journey began in the 1600s in Russia, in the form of one of the most basic mechanical structures—a simple ramp.

In those days people in Russia faced long, cold winters with little to do for fun. Sledding down icy hillsides was one fast and free form of entertainment during the chilly days, but much of the Russian landscape is steppes, flat plains at high altitudes. With no hills to speed down, sledding was not a feasible pastime for most Russians. They solved this problem by erecting frozen slides where natural inclines did not exist. These ramps worked like today's playground slides, only taller and wider. At the bottom of the slope, the ice slides continued for a certain distance, allowing riders to glide to a stop before exiting the ride. "Russian ice slides were built of wood, looking like mammoth skateboard ramps covered with ice," says author and construction expert Spike Carlsen. "One would ascend stairs, hop on a sled, and zing down the 50–degree slope."[1]

Most of the Russian ice slides were built in pairs, each slide next to the other but facing opposite directions. At the end of one slide, riders could get off and immediately be at the stairs of the other slide. When they reached the end of the second slide, they were back at the start of the first, so they could climb and ride in back-and-forth circuits as many times as they wanted.

Ice slides became a very popular form of winter entertainment in Russia, and other European countries eventually learned of their success. The original slides were extremely simple devices, requiring nothing but a ramp and a slick slope. Unfortunately, though the slides were successful in the cold Russian climate, they did not work as well elsewhere. In countries like France, winters were not cold enough to make ice slides a lasting form of entertainment. French inventors were determined to have slides of their own, however, and they solved the problem with a simple mechanical device—wheels. They constructed their own sliding ramps, which looked like the Russian slides but instead of using sleds that glided on ice, the French slides featured small, wheeled carts that rolled down the wooden ramps. To keep the ride's carts on a straight course, designers carved grooved tracks into the wood, which held the carts' wheels. These wheeled carts could be used for year-round fun, making thrill rides no longer just a winter hobby reserved for the coldest climates.

By 1817, the French had made variations on their invention and turned their wheeled ramp rides into major attractions that appealed not just to local residents but also to tourists. One popular ride was named Les Montagnes Russes & Belleville ("the Russian mountains of Belleville"), which allowed two cars to go down the ramp side by side. Another was called the Promenades Aeriennes ("aerial walks"). This slide also allowed two cars to go down at once, though they did not travel side by side. The Promenade Aeriennes was instead shaped like a heart. Riders climbed a single set of steps to reach a common launch point, but then the two tracks diverged, one traveling in a rightward loop, the other going to the left. The curving ramps met at the bottom again and the riders traveled up parallel hills, called lift hills, that took them back to the top of the ride. Wheeled slides like these were impressive structures in their time. "One could reach speeds of 40 miles per hour—in that day the fastest thing on land, air, or sea the average person could ride on,"[2] says Carlsen. The tremendous popularity of these rides proved that people had an appetite for heights, speed, and a sense of daring—ingredients essential for the modern roller coasters to come.

Riding the Rails

While the French were busy thrilling people with their new wheeled rides, across the Atlantic Ocean some American entrepreneurs were discovering their own thrill rides, but more by accident. The young United States was developing into a nation of booming industry, and that industry was run on coal. The substance was plentiful in the hills and mountains throughout the Northeastern United States, and new coal mines were springing up nearly everywhere. The faster a coal company could dig coal out of the mountains and get it downhill to sell it, the more money the company could make.

The traditional method of transporting coal was in carts pulled by mules. In 1827, the Lehigh Coal Mine Company

A rail system was built through Mauch Chunk, Pennsylvania, to allow for the easier transportation of coal through the mountains. Though mules were needed to haul empty carts uphill, the coal they retrieved went down with the railway. The mules traveled down in their own carts, which gave rise to the idea of passenger cars.

built the Mauch Chunk Railway in the Pennsylvania mountains as a faster, easier way to transport cartloads of coal downhill. The rail system and its wheeled carts were the engineering marvel of the day. The track's gentle slope meant gravity, not mules, did the work of carrying the coal downhill, a journey of about 8 miles (13km). Mules rode down in their own specialized carts supplied with food for the journey. At the bottom of the railway, in the town of Mauch Chunk, the mules were let out and harnessed to empty carts. They would haul these back uphill to be reloaded. The animals soon grew accustomed to the ride and eventually refused to go downhill any other way than in a rolling cart.

The transportation of mules perhaps spurred the idea for adding passenger cars to the rails and inviting people to take a ride. The Mauch Chunk Railway started out as a practical solution to a coal transportation problem, but before long it had a different purpose entirely. "In 1872, a large tunnel opened that ended the need for the gravity railroad," says environmental historian Brian Black. "This, however, did not end the gravity line's history." In 1874 the railway was repurposed. "Developers purchased the switchback gravity railroad and made it the centerpiece attraction in Mauch Chunk," Black says, "the tourist attraction of the industrial era."[3] Riders embarked at the top of the railway and enjoyed a scenic downhill trip through the mountains. The gravity-powered ride was far from a daredevil experience, reaching speeds of only 6 miles per hour (10kpm). Nonetheless, it drew huge crowds. About thirty-five thousand people a year flocked to experience the Mauch Chunk Switchback Railway, paying fifty cents per ride (roughly equivalent to ten dollars today). Improvements were made to the attraction over the years, including a cable system that replaced the use of mules to hoist the cars back uphill and a restaurant and hotel to serve visitors. The railway remained in service for fifty-five years, until 1929.

The First Coaster Boom

Though the Mauch Chunk Railway gave a slow and uneventful ride by modern roller coaster standards, it is considered the father of all modern-day coasters. Its basic format—using gravity to roll cars down a train track and a mechanical system to pull the cars back uphill—was the foundation for other roller coasters that emerged once entrepreneurs saw that the earliest tourist rail ride drew visitors by the thousands. A new breed of inventors and engineers came forward who specialized in the creation of thrilling rides.

La Marcus Adna Thompson was one man who took to designing new thrill rides in the late 1800s. His Switchback Railway ride, built in 1884 at Coney Island in Brooklyn, New York, took the Mauch Chunk concept to a new level. "The simple design included a pair of straight, parallel tracks connected at each end by a railroad-type switch," explains roller coaster historians David and Diane Francis. "After negotiating one track, the ride car was 'switched' to the other track for the return trip, thus giving the ride its name."[4] Thompson included rises and drops in his design; instead of rolling along a flat slope, the cars dipped and climbed in a wavelike pattern from one end of the ride to the other. Crowds came out in great numbers to try it. Charging just a nickel a ride, the Switchback Railway made hundreds of dollars a day.

People ride the Switchback Railway ride at Coney Island in 1886. This new ride made the already-popular Coney Island the nation's first amusement park.

The Grandfather of All Coasters

In the 1920s, New York City's Coney Island was a favorite vacation and tourism spot for New Yorkers. It already featured multiple roller coasters and thrill rides, but on June 26, 1927, a new ride opened to the public that forever changed the thrill-ride industry. Standing 85 feet (26m) tall at its highest place and with a track that took a half-mile course (0.8km) through six turnarounds and twelve different drops, the Cyclone set a new standard for roller coasters. Its cars, riding on a wooden track supported by a metal frame, reached 60 miles per hour (97kph) and took riders down a sixty-degree slope—still the seventh-steepest drop of any wooden coaster today. The Cyclone is one of the most famous roller coasters in the world and also an official New York City landmark. It has been copied more times than any roller coaster ever built, with seven other Cyclones operating around the United States, Europe, and Japan. The Cyclone was also placed on the National Register of Historic Places in 1991. Still operating on Coney Island, it is one of the world's oldest rides and widely considered one of the best.

Coney Island was already a popular tourist destination for New Yorkers at the time. It was a nearby getaway where wealthy citizens often went to vacation in fancy hotels. With the addition of the successful Switchback Railway ride, though, the island became the site of the nation's first modern amusement park. New rides were soon invented to compete with the Switchback Railway. In 1884 a designer named Charles Alcoke thought to connect the ends of a coaster track, creating a Coney Island ride that made a complete circuit and ended at the same place it began. In 1885 designer Phillip Hinckle came up with the idea of the mechanized lift hill, an initial slope with a chain that pulled up several cars linked together to form a train. Once cars reached the top of Hinckle's lift hill, they were poised for a steep downward plunge. Hinckle also fashioned ride cars with seats that all faced forward, rather than facing one another as previous ride cars had done. These design adjustments poised roller coasters for a long and successful history. "Since then, dozens of coaster designers have added their own unique twists, turns, adaptations, and alterations, but the fundamental design of the American roller coaster is still the same as it was in 1885,"[5] say the Francises.

New rides sprang up at Coney Island one after another. Patrons paid per ride on each individual coaster. With a dazzling collection of games, coasters, animal performances, and sideshow acts, the experience was like visiting a giant carnival. "There is no accurate census of the number of attractions that were spread over Coney, like a mulch, in the 1920s, but surely there were more than one thousand,"[6] wrote Edo McCullough, son of a Coney Island entrepreneur and a frequent visitor, in 1957.

In 1897 ride owners decided to build a wall around a few rides that were close to each other. Set apart from the others, this group of rides became its own group attraction and was given a theme and a separate name—Sea Lion Park. Historians believe it was the world's first true theme park. Ride designers at Coney Island and elsewhere soon followed the trend of clustering rides together within walled spaces filled with particular, sometimes themed, attractions and food. Thomas Edison's introduction of electric light bulbs in the late 1800s gave some of these parks an enthralling after-dark glow. By the turn of the twentieth century, an exciting era of theme parks was under way.

The Coaster Craze Goes National

The boom in roller coasters was not just confined to New York. It rapidly spread around the United States, taking root in metropolises like Chicago, as well as smaller cities. Americans everywhere loved roller coasters and paid to ride them. Faced with the promise of a very popular and profitable industry, roller coaster entrepreneurs built new rides and created theme parks all around the country.

A trolley travels on a rail down a street in San Francisco in the late nineteenth century. The popularity of roller coasters led to the creation of trolley parks that carried people around town on tracks laid into flat pavement.

The coaster craze gave a needed boost to the economies of many smaller cities and towns in the form of trolley parks. Trolleys, also known as streetcars or cable cars, carried groups of people through a city or town on a track embedded in the paved street surface. The track contained a cable that rotated continuously, similar to how a conveyor belt operates. The cable hooked to the underside of a cable car and could tow it from one place to another. A massive steam engine, usually located on the outskirts of town at the start or end of the trolley line, powered the cable's movement. The first trolleys were invented for the steep, hilly streets of San Francisco in 1871, replacing horse- or mule-towed wagons. By the early 1900s, cable-car systems were used in many other cities as a quick, cost-effective way for people to get around town.

Trolleys were usually crowded during the workweek, but in many cities they sat empty on weekends. Businesspeople realized that if they could build exciting attractions on the outskirts of their cities, they could get paying riders onto the trolleys every Saturday and Sunday for a ride to the entertainment destination. Roller coasters provided exactly the draw the cable car companies needed. So-called trolley

Coaster Fan Club

In 1978 a group of roller coaster fans formed a club called American Coaster Enthusiasts (ACE), with the mission of supporting roller coasters of all kinds and especially preserving historic wooden coasters in the United States. The organization is now five thousand members strong. It publishes *RollerCoaster!* magazine and a series of coaster guidebooks, and its website contains information about coasters all around the world. Since its creation, ACE has also been instrumental in preserving historic roller coasters such as Leap-the-Dips at Lakemont Park in Pennsylvania. Built in 1902, Leap-the-Dips is the oldest operating wooden coaster and the world's only remaining coaster with side-friction wheels. In exchange for their preservation efforts, members of ACE receive discounted admission prices at many U.S. amusement parks. ACE sponsors multiple national and regional events and conventions at amusement parks each year, and those who attend are often allowed into a park before or after hours to experience rides without the normal crowds.

ACE membership is open to anyone with a love of coasters. Members pay annual dues that help support the organization's mission to protect and preserve roller coasters. More information about ACE can be found at its website: www.aceonline.org.

parks opened up on the outer edges of many American cities, right where the trolley lines ended. In the early 1900s, many Americans spent their money and leisure time at trolley parks, enjoying multiple fun attractions there but mainly riding roller coasters.

Modernized Mechanisms

American theme parks and trolley parks made roller coasters a national phenomenon. By the 1920s, an estimated fifteen hundred to two thousand of the structures towered around the nation. New engineers were coming up with mechanical devices that made it possible to construct ever bigger, faster, and more exciting rides, and John A. Miller was among these inventors. Considered one of history's most influential coaster designers, Miller improved ride designs with inventions like an antirollback device, a toothed contraption that ran along the track of the lift hill. Every time

ROLLER COASTER NATION

With a startling 648 roller coasters (as of March 2012) the United States has more coasters than any other country in the world.

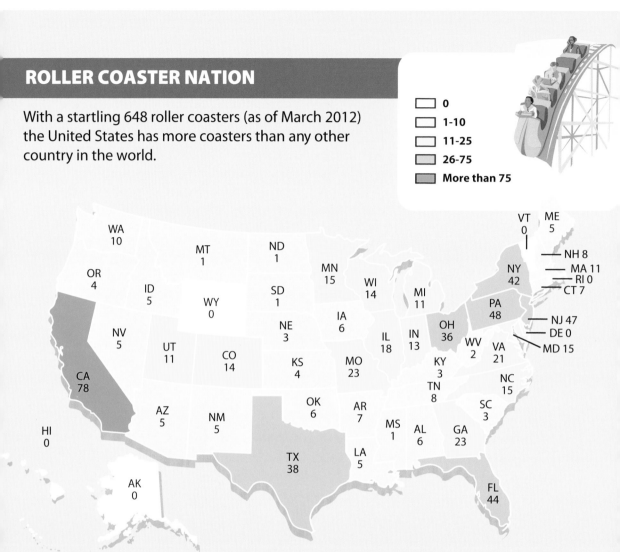

Legend:
- 0
- 1-10
- 11-25
- 26-75
- More than 75

WA 10
OR 4
ID 5
MT 1
ND 1
MN 15
WI 14
MI 11
NY 42
VT 0
ME 5
NH 8
MA 11
RI 0
CT 7
NV 5
UT 11
WY 0
SD 1
NE 3
IA 6
IL 18
IN 13
OH 36
WV 2
VA 21
PA 48
NJ 47
DE 0
MD 15
CA 78
AZ 5
NM 5
CO 14
KS 4
MO 23
OK 6
AR 7
KY 3
TN 8
NC 15
SC 3
MS 1
AL 6
GA 23
TX 38
LA 5
HI 0
AK 0
FL 44

Source: Roller Coaster Census Report, reported by the Roller Coaster Database.
http://www.rcdb.com/census.htm?l=59.

the car was pulled up the hill another foot or so, a hook on its underside would catch the next antirollback tooth, making it impossible for the car to slide backward during its ascent. (This device is responsible for the rhythmic clanking noise that has become iconic on the lift hills of many coasters.)

The antirollback device made higher lift hills possible while improving coaster safety.

Miller also invented underfriction wheels, coaster wheels that rolled along the underside of a train's steel track instead of along the top of it. This design ensured that the cars firmly gripped the track at all times. They made it possible for rides to include sudden, steep dips that would have caused top-gripping wheels to fly right off the tracks. Miller's improvements allowed him to design and build coasters that were faster and wilder than any before them. According to the Francises, he was "among the designers who helped transform the early, sedate roller coaster into a modern sky-scraping, high-speed thriller."[7] In the 1920s, Miller's steep-dropping, fast-dipping track designs launched roller coasters to soaring new heights of excitement and possibility. "Without John

The development of under-friction wheels allowed roller coasters to handle sudden, steep dips without flying off the tracks.

Continental Coasters

Modern roller coasters were an American innovation, but the roller coaster craze has long since gone global. Amusement parks and roller coasters are found on six of the world's seven continents. They have become especially numerous in Asian countries. Host to more than eleven hundred active roller coasters, Asia has over a third of all the world's thrill rides. Europe and North America, combined, boast another fifteen hundred. Africa, with only forty-three roller coasters, has the second fewest of any continent (with Australia having the least, at twenty-five) but nevertheless has bragging rights with rides like the Cobra at Ratanga Junction Theme Park in South Africa. Amusement parks are popular tourist destinations that can generate valuable income, and roller coasters are almost every park's most popular attraction. Even in developing nations where coasters are few, amusement parks and their roller coasters can be a valuable source of tourism revenue that gives a boost to the local economy.

Miller's inventions, we would not have the wild thrill rides of today," says roller coaster and theme park historian Steven J. Urbanowicz, adding, "With the advent of Miller's inventions, any type of design could now be executed."[8] Miller made rides safer than ever, too. Almost a century after being built, some of Miller's coasters still operate today—among them the Big Dipper at Six Flags Worlds of Adventure near Cleveland, Ohio. Old as this ride is, it has one of the best safety records of all the coasters in history.

The Boom Busts

By the 1920s, roller coasters and amusement parks were an industry all their own. Whenever people had spending money, they often wanted to spend it on roller coaster rides. The market for this new type of entertainment was huge, spawning thousands of new coasters. During the 1920s, an era during which Americans were celebrating feelings of

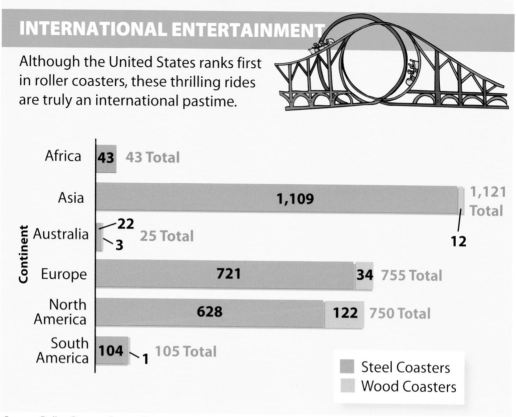

INTERNATIONAL ENTERTAINMENT

Although the United States ranks first in roller coasters, these thrilling rides are truly an international pastime.

Continent

- Africa: 43 — 43 Total
- Asia: 1,109 — 1,121 Total
- Australia: 22 / 3 — 25 Total — 12
- Europe: 721 — 34 — 755 Total
- North America: 628 — 122 — 750 Total
- South America: 104 — 1 — 105 Total

Steel Coasters
Wood Coasters

Source: Roller Coaster Census Report, as recorded by the Roller Coaster Database. http://www.rcdb.com/census.htm.

freedom, fun, and prosperity, roller coasters enjoyed a heyday as an outrageously popular leisure-time fad.

All that ended when the American stock market crashed in 1929, setting off the greatest economic crisis in U.S. history. The national period of hardship that followed is known as the Great Depr ession. Many Americans lost their jobs and even their homes. Few people had spare money to spend on frivolous pastimes like roller coaster rides. Coasters' popularity came crashing down and many of the rides were dismantled so that their wood and steel could be reused. Most amusement parks, formerly ablaze with light, music, and happy crowds, shut down and fell into disrepair.

For more than two decades, the United States largely forgot about its former roller coaster fad. The Great Depression came to an end, and life improved economically, but then the

United States went to war. From 1941 to 1945, the nation's involvement in World War II kept people's thoughts turned toward more serious matters such as constructing battleships and providing war supplies. Designing and building amusement park rides was no longer a priority.

The Coaster Comes Back

When World War II ended, prosperity and optimism returned to the United States, but roller coaster rides mostly remained historical relics from decades past. It took a new kind of park and a new kind of ride to kick-start the industry again. Americans had developed a love of movies, and by the 1950s, many people had television sets in their homes. Cartoon characters that were the brainstorm of a man named Walt Disney had become powerful American icons. Mickey Mouse, Donald Duck, and their many animated friends were household names. Wanting to expand his entertainment empire, Disney looked to the past and the long-forgotten idea of a theme park. Hoping to combine this concept with the already booming success of his company's cartoon characters, he hired people to design and build a brand-new theme park in Southern California. It opened in 1955. He called it Disneyland.

The highly anticipated new theme park was the first in the world to base its popularity on the film industry, but Disney did not want to stop there. He constantly improved and expanded the park, wanting to include rides that could take people back to an era when physical thrills had dominated the leisure industry. In 1959 Disneyland opened the gates to a new attraction—a roller coaster called the Matterhorn Bobsleds. Unlike its railway-inspired ancestors, this thrill voyage did not operate on clunky rails or sit high on a monstrous meshwork of wooden stilts and crosspieces. Instead, "bobsleds" wove in and out of a replica of Switzerland's famed alpine peak the Matterhorn on two curving steel rails.

BITS & BYTES

50%

Percentage of the world's top ten most-visited amusement parks that are in the United States

The fourteen-story ride plunged passengers down steep hills, in and out of mountain caves, and around sharply banked turns. It splashed through pools of water and slid just beneath the clutches of a terrifying abominable snowman. The hair-raising tour was visible to awed spectators watching from the ground outside, and shrieks of delight—and perhaps terror—echoed through the mountain's caverns before each bobsled came to a halt and the passengers safely emerged, flushed and grinning, to exit the ride on wobbly knees.

Disneyland's Matterhorn Bobsleds was the first ride of its kind, a rollicking twister that traveled on steel tubes instead of train rails. "A true innovation in engineering and construction, the Matterhorn Bobsleds became the first modern all-steel coaster, using a tubular track and nylon wheels on the trains," says coaster enthusiast and researcher Todd Throgmorton. With the Matterhorn Bobsleds, Disneyland reignited America's appetite for thrill rides and launched a generation of coasters like none the world had ever seen—ones that traveled on tubular steel track pieces welded

Disneyland's Matterhorn Bobsled ride, which opened in 1959, was the first ride to use steel tubes instead of train rails. It helped launch a public appetite for more thrilling rides.

Wooden Wonders

Most of the world's modern coasters are steel, addressing riders' preferences for a smoother, faster ride. Only in the United States, where the modern roller coaster phenomenon began and owes its legacy to the wooden models, do wooden coasters continue to enjoy great popularity. Of the 172 wooden coasters that operate around the world, 122 of them are in North America, according to the Roller Coaster Database. Modern wooden coasters may lack some of the newfangled features made possible by the addition of steel, but they are not merely nostalgic relics of the past, either. These coasters provide some of the steepest, gut-wrenching drops to be found on any roller coaster today. Son of Beast at Kings Island in Ohio, for example, drops riders down a 214-foot slope (65m) and reaches speeds of close to 80 miles per hour (130kph). Today's amusement parks are filled with hard-to-satisfy thrill seekers, but wooden coasters are still white-knuckle rides. The uniquely American structures are the pride and joy of many American amusement parks.

together for a seamless ride. "This ride became the basis for a new breed of coasters," says Throgmorton, enabling designers "to build spirals and turns not feasible with wooden tracks."[9] Disneyland's signature coaster set in motion a new roller coaster frenzy that took the United States, and later the world, by storm. Thrill rides have remained popular ever since.

Modern-Day Coasters

Steel coaster designs provide a far different riding experience than the wooden behemoths that came before them. Steel tracks are fashioned into sometimes elegant but often daredevil sections that are seamlessly welded together and can curve, twist, cross over and under each other, and flip riders upside down. The paths a steel coaster can take are limitless. The ride, compared with the clattering and jolting of wooden coasters, is smooth, quiet, fast, and often terrifying. Steel coasters break new boundaries every year and are responsible for the coaster phenomenon's spread to every inhabited continent. Wooden coasters have not fallen entirely by the wayside, however. They have unique charm and offer their own thrilling heights and designs. But in steel

The Son of Beast roller coaster ride at Kings Island in Ohio is a huge structure built of wood instead of steel. Though most coasters today are constructed of steel, wooden coasters remain popular.

coasters, the worlds of science and technology have come together to create thrill-ride phenomena that see few limitations. If the human mind can imagine it, today's coaster engineers can probably design it.

CHAPTER 2

How Coasters Roll: The Physics of the Coaster Phenomenon

Given the trailblazing developments in modern roller coasters, it is sometimes easy to forget that all rides owe their existence to the designs that came before them. Today's coasters may be massive towers of twisting tubular steel, but any coaster, regardless of its size, speed, or terror-generating power, is ultimately a descendent of those early Russian ice slides. It was there that human ingenuity came up with the idea of building these unique venues for using gravity for fun. This simple idea is still the chief law of roller coaster technology.

Roller coasters have the appearance of being very complex mechanical contraptions. The more they twist, turn, and flip and the faster they go, the more they seem to defy the laws of physics. In actuality, roller coasters thrive on these basic laws and owe their existence to them. A roller coaster is considered any elevated track with curves and rises, carrying passengers in open, rolling cars for entertainment. The cars of a roller coaster have no onboard motor, yet they can reach speeds that exceed freeway limits for automobiles while rolling along tracks that curve, twist, rise, and plunge. They do it all by capitalizing on the same natural force that the Mauch

Calculating Coaster Slopes

Every sloping surface has a measure of steepness based on its rise over run, or the change in its height over a given length. A slope can be thought of as part of a right triangle. The length of the vertical side is the rise. The length of the horizontal side is the run. The third line, the hypotenuse, has a slope measured as the ratio between the height and the length of the triangle.

The slope of any segment of a roller coaster track can be found by drawing a vertical line down from the segment's upper endpoint and a horizontal line across from the lower endpoint. These three lines form a right triangle, giving the measurements needed to calculate slope. If the rise and run are equal, meaning for every 1 unit of measurement in rise, 1 unit is also covered in length, the slope will be 45 degrees. The larger the degree measurement, the steeper the slope. In 2011 the world record for the steepest roller coaster was set by Takabisha at Fuji-Q Highland Amusement Park in Japan. The ride has a slope measuring 121 degrees—it is steeper than vertical, actually sending riders partially upside-down.

Chunk Railway used in the 1800s for its far gentler downhill ride—gravity.

What Goes Up Must Come Down

The main principle underlying all roller coaster technology is one of the most basic natural forces in the universe. Everything in the world that can be touched and takes up space is made of matter, and everything made of matter has mass—a measure of the amount of matter contained in an object of a certain size. All things that have mass are pulled toward one another. This force pulling matter toward other matter is called gravity. The more mass an object has, the greater its pull on the things around it. Very massive things such as the sun pull on smaller things such as planets more strongly than the planets pull back on them. The mutual pulling force of gravity keeps the earth and the other planets of our solar system revolving around the sun. The same force keeps the moon in orbit around the earth. Because it is smaller, the moon is pulled more strongly toward the earth than vice

Gravity is the main principle behind roller coaster technology. It is gravity's pulling force that keeps planets like the earth and moon traveling around the sun.

versa, but it does exert its own gravitational pull on the earth, too. This is why the oceans have tides: The moon's gravity pulls water toward or away from the shorelines throughout a cycle of day and night.

The earth's mass is much larger than the moon's, and it absolutely dwarfs objects that exist on its surface. A person has mass and thus creates his or her own gravity that pulls slightly against the earth. But because the planet has tremendous mass compared with a human body, a person's pull on the earth is negligible, while the earth's gravitational pull on people keeps their feet planted firmly on the ground. It is very difficult to defy the force of gravity. A person can jump into the air, but the instant her feet leave the ground, gravity is already pulling her back down. The constant tug of the earth against anything with mass that tries to leave its surface is the primary force that makes all roller coasters go. "Virtually all roller coasters are slaves to one very common attribute: gravity," says roller coaster enthusiast and author Scott Rutherford. "The roller coaster is a perfect illustration of the concept that what goes up will, in all likelihood, eventually come down. On a roller coaster, this usually occurs quite rapidly, and that's a major reason why we ride the things in the first place."[10]

Gravity Gives Rise to Energy

To understand how roller coasters work, it is important to know that gravity does not really pull things toward the *surface* of the earth. Since the planet is a sphere, gravity is actually pulling all objects toward the *center* of the earth. It is only because things cannot pass through the earth itself that they come to a halt on its surface. If it is ever possible for something to get closer to the center of the earth, gravity works to make it happen. Objects placed at the top of a sloped surface always tend to slide or roll down to the bottom, for example, because the bottom is nearer to the planet's center. Seventeenth-century Russian ice slides worked because of this principle. A wooden slope raised riders off the earth's surface, allowing them to slide from a high point to a lower one. Gravity always pulls things straight down if it can, but if something like a slope stands in the way of a straight fall, gravity will at least pull things down the slope, as long as that will bring the object closer to the earth's center.

The earth is always pulling against anything that tries to get away from its core, so energy is needed to overcome gravity.

During a ride, a roller coaster car experiences several shifts in potential energy and kinetic energy. At the top of a high hill – such as a lift hill – the car will have no kinetic energy because it is not moving, but will have a high stored potential energy. As the car moves to the bottom of a hill, amounts of potential and kinetic energy will shift, with kinetic energy increasing as the car moves, and potential energy decreasing.

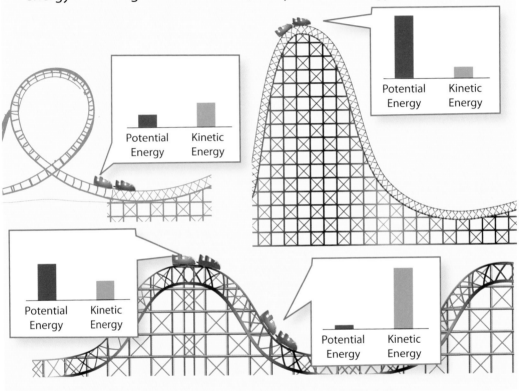

Walking uphill is harder than walking downhill, for example, because it means walking away from the center of the earth, against the gravitational pull. The steeper the hill, the harder it is to walk up it because it takes more energy to overcome the pull of gravity. Energy is the basic ability of an object to do work, which, in physics, is defined as pushing or pulling against something else. "In order to lift an object or even to climb stairs, the body must expend energy to overcome the

Becoming a Roller Coaster Engineer

Job Description: Roller coaster engineers come up with the technical designs for new roller coasters. They decide on track length and height; car design; features like curves, drops, and turns; and launching and braking mechanisms. They work closely with park managers, other engineers, and construction crews. They may also be involved in ongoing maintenance of the rides they have designed.

Education: A minimum of a bachelor's degree in engineering (usually mechanical engineering) is required. Many roller coaster engineers have a master's degree. A professional engineer (PE) designation may be necessary to find a job in this field. Practical experience in roller coaster operations and design, such

as through an internship or summer employment, improves job prospects.

Qualifications: In addition to a solid background in engineering and the operation of amusement parks, roller coaster engineers must be creative and have good teamwork and leadership skills. Flexibility and good problem-solving skills are also important, as are good written and spoken communication skills.

Additional Information: Roller coaster projects and engineering companies are located all over the world, so engineers should be willing to travel or even relocate to other areas when the job requires.

Salary: About $44,000 to $100,000 per year or more.

force of gravity,"[11] says physics professor Richard McCall. At the top of the hill, a hiker probably has to stop and rest a while, but the energy expended to move to the top of the hill—called kinetic energy, or the energy of an object in motion—has not been wasted. The hiker sitting on the top of the hill now has another type of energy: potential energy. "An object with potential energy has the *potential* to do work, even if it is not currently doing work," says McCall. "Another way to think of potential energy is that it is stored energy or stored work."[12]

A hiker expends energy to overcome the force of gravity, but at the top of the hill, the force of gravity wants to pull him to the bottom again. This creates potential energy. If the hill is snowy or icy, and if the hiker happens to have a sled to sit on, his potential (stored) energy at the top of the hill can be let loose. As long as the sled is smooth and glides easily against the snow (creating little friction, or the slowing force generated when the surface of one object slides against the surface of another), all the hiker must do is point the sled downhill. Gravity will do the rest. The potential energy the hiker built during the uphill climb becomes kinetic energy once he is plummeting back downhill due to the force of gravity.

Every roller coaster relies on these principles of gravity, potential energy, and kinetic energy. The Mauch Chunk Railway built potential energy as mules pulled the train's passenger cars uphill. At the top of the hill, people climbed aboard, and the potential (stored) energy was released as gravity pulled the cars back down the sloped track to its lowest point. Coasters have only gotten more exciting since then as designers have played with the idea of how to defy gravity to build potential energy, then let gravity change potential energy to kinetic energy as the cars plummet back downhill. The long lift hill at the start of almost any modern coaster ride is really a way to build potential energy. Once the ride's cars are at the top of the hill, they seem to explode into motion. The taller the hill, the more energy it takes to overcome gravity and get the cars to the top—but they then have more potential energy, too. "The higher the object, the larger the gravitational potential energy," says McCall. "An object 10m above the ground has ten times more potential energy than an object only 1m above the ground."[13] High lift hills promise a fast, hair-raising coaster ride.

Meeting a Coaster's Potential

All roller coasters—even the twistiest, curviest, and most daring—play by the same physical rules involving potential energy, kinetic energy, gravity, and momentum. Yet, coasters have experienced a tremendous technical evolution over the years, too. Long gone are the days of using mules' energy to pull coaster cars up a rise. Today's coaster designers have developed advanced techniques for building potential energy by sending cars up a lift hill.

The chain lift is the oldest mechanical method for reaching the top of a lift hill, and it is still one of the most common. A long loop of heavy chain runs under the track from the bottom of the lift hill to the top. Gears at the bottom and

the top of the hill are run by a motor. These gears grip the chain and turn it to keep the loop in constant motion, working like a conveyor belt. Sturdy, hinged hooks on the bottom of each roller coaster car latch onto the links of the moving chain. Once attached, the motorized chain mechanism pulls the train up the lift hill. At the top, the train unhooks so that it can plunge down the back side of the lift hill.

Some rides use cable lifts instead of chains to get a car up the lift hill. In a cable lift system, a thick, sturdy cable runs along the track beneath the train of coaster cars. Attached to the cable is a hook that grabs onto the bottom of the ride's cars. The cable is connected to a winch at one end, a device that works like a spool; when a motor turns the winch, it rapidly winds up the cable. As the cable gets wound at one end, it pulls the train of passenger cars up the lift hill, similar to the way an elevator lifts a load of passengers up an elevator shaft. Cable lifts provide a smoother and often much faster alternative to

A workman tends to chain on a roller coaster track at Coney Island in 1936. The chain lift was originally used to propel roller coasters to the top of a lift hill.

Upgrade: Tilt Lifts

A typical roller coaster lift hill takes riders up a slope. The cars crest the top of the hill one at a time, then start the descent. The train picks up speed gradually because it has to wait for all of its cars to crest the hill before it can reach its full downhill velocity. A tilt lift is a different approach to the standard lift hill. In this design, a train of cars is pulled up a lift hill, but when it reaches the top, the entire train is moved onto a horizontal platform. A hook attaches to the back of the train to keep it from rolling forward and off the platform. The platform is then tilted forward, pointing all riders downhill at the same time. When the hook is released, the train moves onto a nearly vertical section of track, beginning its ride through the rest of the coaster. There is only one operating tilt-lift coaster in the world—Gravity Max at Six Flags Discovery World in Taiwan—but this innovative approach to the traditional lift hill creates a new dimension of terror for those who squirm at heights.

a traditional chain lift. The motor that turns the winch is also extremely powerful. Some cable lifts wind so quickly that they yank passenger trains forward, creating almost instantaneous speed, before propelling them to the top of the lift hill.

However a roller coaster accomplishes its initial ascent, the potential energy at the crest of a hill is what makes the rest of the ride possible. "All you have to understand is gravity and the conversion between two different kinds of energy—potential and kinetic," says physicist Amy Lytle. "All the energy that you get in the ride is really from that initial lift hill."[14] These forces keep the coaster sailing through every successive lift, loop, and twist the ride provides.

A Coaster in Motion Stays in Motion

The Mauch Chunk Railway and Russian ice slides used potential and kinetic energy the simplest possible way: energy was expended to get uphill, and then gravity was used to get back down. At the bottom of the slope, the ride was over. These early attempts at rides were fun, but modern coaster enthusiasts seek greater thrills from a ride. Most of today's coasters build potential energy multiple times during a single ride. They are not straight, downhill slopes. Instead, they often have multiple hills, each rise taking the coaster's cars and riders away from the ground only to plummet them down again. From the top of the first lift hill, there is not a slow moment for the rest of the ride.

Roller coasters use gravity and potential energy to get going initially, but what keeps them moving is another fundamental law of physics. This law states that any object at rest will stay at rest unless something acts on it to move it and that any object, once in motion, will stay in motion unless an outside force acts on it to stop it. This property of matter is called inertia. Sir Isaac Newton, a famous seventeenth-century physicist, was the first person to study and define this natural phenomenon, so it is called Newton's first law of motion. This law is important for roller coasters because it means that a coaster car, once moving, will tend to continue going forward along the track as long as no force stops it. This is because a roller coaster car has inertia—a natural resistance of any object with mass to any change in its motion. According to Newton's first law of motion, if the car is still, its inertia will keep it still in the absence of any outside force to move it, but once it is moving, it will similarly stay moving unless an outside force interferes. It takes force to overcome inertia (a roller coaster car needs a mechanical "push" to get up the lift hill), but once an object is in motion, inertia also works to keep it that way.

Roller coasters are also governed by another physical principle, momentum, or the measure of any moving object's motion. The momentum of an object can be found by multiplying the mass of the moving object by the velocity, or rate of speed, at which it is moving. The heavier an object and the faster it is moving, the more momentum it has. Roller coaster trains, when filled with passengers, have the potential to develop a great deal of momentum. Getting them up to a high speed, or velocity, means they will then tend to continue moving at a high speed due to inertia. A coaster car that has just plummeted down the backside of the lift hill on a track has enough momentum to push it up the next hill. Gravity will work against the car and may even slow it down somewhat, but the car's momentum will do the work of pushing it forward even against the force of gravity, getting it up and over the crest of the next hill. Then it will build even more momentum as it goes down the second hill. Momentum is why coaster cars do not need onboard energy generators such as motors and why coaster tracks tend to have so many steep hills and dips. The momentum a train of cars builds on downhill slopes propels it and its passengers through the whole ride.

Bending the Tracks

Because of momentum, coaster cars can keep going up one hill and down the other at high speeds. The early Switchback Railway ride at Coney Island worked this way, rolling up and down hills from one end of the straight track to the other. Today's coaster rides, however, are anything but straight. They twist, coil, and even turn riders upside down, pulling passengers into exciting and unexpected patterns of curves and bends. Just as momentum keeps cars moving forward along the track, it also drives them through these snakelike patterns. Putting a sharp turn into a track that will carry a fast-moving train of cars is tricky, however, because a moving object's natural tendency is not only to keep moving, but to keep moving in the direction it is already going. Unless acted on by some outside force that changes its direction, a roller coaster car will naturally keep moving forward. Wherever the track bends, the laws of physics make the coaster car go straight. Cars, therefore, must cling firmly to a track throughout the entire ride to keep from flying off course; that is, off the track.

Wheels of modern coasters grip the track in all directions. Coaster designer John Miller invented wheels that wrapped around the track to grip

BITS & BYTES

1.6 million feet (488,000m)

Combined length of wood pieces needed to build the American Eagle, a wooden coaster in Illinois it from underneath so that cars stayed put during steep drops and dips. Today's cars, especially on curvy steel coasters, have wheels that also grip the inside and outside of the rails. This way, when the track veers suddenly to the left or the right, the cars stay firmly attached to it. The wheel mechanisms overcome the car's natural tendency to go straight, and the cars hold firmly to the track throughout its curvy course. "Even today's modern steel coasters use a version of Miller's pioneering vision to keep the lightning-fast trains on course and anchored to the track,"[15] says Rutherford.

It is also important when designing a ride to ensure that the riders, whose bodies are objects in motion as well, and naturally want to go straight, are kept in the coaster cars. Seatbelts, lap bars, and on some rides, even padded over-the-shoulder harnesses keep passengers firmly and safely in place around all of the ride's rollicking turns and twists. Wheels and passenger restraints are designed to defy the laws of physics and allow roller coaster riders to safely move in anything but a straight line.

Living Through the Loop

Momentum and the natural tendency of a moving object to continue moving in a straight line also make possible the famed inversion, or loop-the-loop—a track feature that turns cars and their riders upside down as their path completes the shape of a circle. Loop-the-loop designs seem to defy basic natural phenomena like gravity. Logic suggests that at the top of the loop, a coaster car should fall straight down. If the car were not moving with enough velocity and were not securely attached to the track by its wheels, this might happen. But the car builds momentum through the use of hills and gravity during the ride and is moving fast when it starts its journey into a successful inversion. The shape of the track forces the car to travel in an upward curve when its natural tendency would be to keep moving forward. The car's inertia, or resistance to a change in its straightforward motion, fights the upward path the track forces it to take. The car strives to keep going forward instead of up and over, and will push outward against the curving shape of the track.

CENTRIPETAL FORCE AND THE LOOP

Centripetal force is the force that pushes or pulls an object moving on a curved path towards the center of its rotation. When a child swings a ball on a string, for instance, the ball wants to move straight, following its path of inertia, but the force exerted by the string keeps it moving in a circle. In a loop of roller coaster track, the train and its passengers are pushed towards the center of rotation by the force of the tracks on the roller coaster cars.

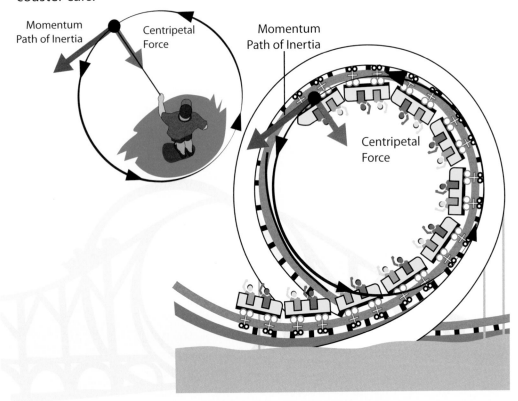

Momentum Path of Inertia

Centripetal Force

Momentum Path of Inertia

Centripetal Force

This phenomenon is called centripetal force; the cars would normally go straight, but the track forces them in a different direction, so they push against whatever constraint forces them to travel in a circle. It is the same concept that makes riders slide to the outer edges of a merry-go-round.

The faster the platform spins, the more momentum the riders' bodies have and the stronger their natural tendency to go in a straight line. Riders are pressed against the bars on the outer rim of the merry-go-round while it spins, and if they do not hang on, they will be flung off (and then travel in a straight line until they hit the ground). Centripetal force also helps keep roller coaster cars tight against the track, and riders tight in their seats, during an inversion.

A Better Kind of Loop

A favorite roller coaster feature is an inversion, when the track goes upward and turns cars completely upside down before descending. The maneuver is commonly called a loop, but modern coaster loops are not perfectly circular. Instead, they look as if a circle has been stretched upward at the top, a shape known as a clothoid loop. Coasters use this design instead of a perfect circle, because to travel through a circular loop without losing momentum at the top, coaster cars have to be moving very fast going into the loop. Surging into a sharp curve at high speed puts tremendous gravitational, or "g," forces (between six and twelve g's; i.e., six–twelve time the normal force of gravity) on human passengers, enough to make many people lose consciousness. In clothoid loops, however, coasters move more straight up and down than they would in a circular curve. Passengers fare much better on these loops than they did on early looped-track designs. The first roller coaster loops, some of which appeared in Europe as early as the 1840s, caused harsh whiplash for some passengers and made others pass out. Coasters eventually abandoned loops altogether until designers perfected the clothoid loop in the 1970s. Today, there are coaster tracks that feature as many as eleven such inversions during a single ride.

"The track is constantly pushing the car in a new direction," says chemist and science writer Steve Miller. "The seat of the car pushes you in the same direction. Your own inertia tends to keep you moving in a straight line away from the center of the circle . . . but the car is pushing against you to prevent it." As long as the car keeps moving quickly, centripetal force presses riders so firmly into their seats that they cannot fall out as they complete the upside-down loop. "Even without a safety harness, you would stay in the car,"[16] says Miller.

Energetic Builders

Although the momentum created by gravity does the majority of a roller coaster's physical work, successful ride designs do not happen by accident. One look at a towering mountain of wooden supports or a metal track whose brightly painted rails resemble a giant bowl of spaghetti suggests that designing and building a modern coaster is a huge undertaking. Designers want each coaster to give riders an experience new and different from any other coaster they may have ridden. To accomplish this goal, they combine physics with engineering principles to create expensive, complicated technological marvels, the main purpose of which is to let people have fun.

Roller coasters may send riders into an inversion, putting them upside down in the coaster cars. Inversions created by loops were abandoned for awhile due to safety problems, but returned when technology was able to correct those problems.

CHAPTER 3

From Blueprint to Ride: Building a Coaster

R oller coasters work by pushing chains of cars to the top of a hill, then letting gravity and momentum carry the cars and their riders through the rest of the track's turns, dips, and loops. Every ride is a partnership between the chain of cars and the track it is coasting on. To ensure a fun and safe voyage for riders, every inch of a track must be carefully designed, built, and tested. Turning an idea for a new ride into an actual, physical roller coaster requires thorough knowledge of physics to predict how the coaster's cars will behave while in motion. It also requires equal knowledge of construction materials and techniques that will result in a sturdy and properly functioning structure. Building a new roller coaster is a major and expensive undertaking. Those who create coaster designs and those who actually build the coasters work together to turn great ideas into towering rides without making mistakes that could require costly repairs and rebuilding. No roller coaster designer works entirely from scratch. All designers try to create coasters with new elements the world has not seen, but at the same time, they usually also simply tweak or improve on basic coaster design elements that have been used before.

Getting Ideas

Every new roller coaster design is based solidly on what worked well in the past and what is working well in other coasters today. Designers are equally creative and competitive, trying to come up with rides unlike any that have been built before, and they are also well aware of what other designers have done and are doing. Engineers and designers are always looking for new ways to use common coaster elements like steep drops, loops, and twisting

The Kingda Ka roller coaster at Six Flags Great Adventure in New Jersey is the tallest and fastest coaster in the world.

Where Does Energy Go?

As a roller coaster climbs the first lift hill of its track, it is building potential energy—the higher it gets above the earth, the stronger the pull of gravity will be. When the coaster crests the lift hill and begins its descent, its potential energy becomes kinetic energy, or the energy of movement. A common misperception is that a coaster loses energy along the track. An important law of physics, however, called the law of conservation of energy, is that energy can never be created nor destroyed. It simply changes from one form to another. Whenever a track rises back uphill, the cars' momentum—their kinetic energy—will carry them upward, which builds potential energy. Roller coasters repeatedly convert potential energy to kinetic energy and back again.

At the end of a ride, coaster cars are slowed down by brake mechanisms that create friction. Friction between two surfaces makes them hot, meaning kinetic energy is changed to heat energy during braking. Riders may mistakenly think coasters lose energy at the end of the track, but the energy is never lost nor created. It just changes to and from different forms.

sections of track in a combination that will make a fun new ride.

Though designers try to be creative, certain elements are a fundamental part of any roller coaster design, and different designers take different approaches to these features. The initial lift hill, for example, is a necessity for any coaster, to create enough initial potential energy to generate the momentum needed for the coaster cars to complete the course. Some designers plan to get riders to the top of the lift hill as quickly as possible so that they can plunge downward to the other things the coaster has in store—perhaps a record number of loops or an innovative design for a twisting loop. Other designers deliberately plan for a long, slow ascent up the lift hill, one that builds suspense among riders as well as energy. In some rides, the lift hill basically *is* the ride. The Kingda Ka at Six Flags Great Adventure in New Jersey, for example, famously broke records for being the tallest and fastest roller coaster in the world. But it does little more than send riders to the crest of a terrifying 456-foot (139m) lift hill before letting them plummet, face-first, toward the ground at up to 128 miles per hour (206kph).

Whatever the main drawing attraction of a particular ride may be, they all require an investment of careful planning and calculation on the part of the designer. The process of designing a coaster begins with choosing the type of riders the track is built for—considering, for example, their age, size, and expected tolerance for speed and motion—and also how they will be situated in the cars as they move around the track. This will determine the shape a coaster will take and what kind of lifts, loops, and curves its track can make. "First, the park comes to us and gives us a general idea of what they want," says Sandor Kernacs, president of a worldwide roller coaster engineering firm called Intamin. "The engineers and I then come up with a concept that we present to the park. We then have discussions of what changes to make to it, and we talk about whether we have the technologies to address what we came up with. . . . But it starts with the conceptual design—that's the most important part."[17]

Types of Coaster Car

A new ride's possibilities and limits depend largely on the type of car it will use and the cars' placement on the track. Early roller coaster cars attached to the track along the bottom of the car and seated guests side-by-side, usually in pairs, in forward-facing seats. The cars traveled on two parallel rails. Many of today's coasters, especially the wooden ones, stick to this same tried-and-true format of car design. The advent of steel roller coasters, however, made it possible to create different and more creative designs, as well as new styles of cars to take advantage of the possibilities. The original sit-down cars with wheels on the bottom have now been joined by a wide new array of coaster vehicles.

With the development of the over-the-shoulder harness, riders were able to stand up or experience a ride without the sides of a car surrounding them.

Some coasters have replaced the two-rail system with a single rail that runs beneath the car, making the riding experience feel like floating through the air because the rail itself is out of the passengers' direct line of sight. Other coaster cars are designed so that riders stand up, straddling a bench-like cushion for support and holding onto an over-the-shoulder harness. Many modern coasters have also flipped the standard car design upside-down. Called suspended or inverted coasters, the track on these rides is above the cars instead of below them. The cars attach to the underside of the track, sometimes allowing the seated riders' feet to dangle and the cars to swing from side to side as they surge around the bends. Still other designs position riders so that they lie face-down with their bodies supported at the shoulders, chest, waist, knees, and feet. They look at the ground throughout the ride, which is intended to simulate the feeling of flying superhero-style through the air. Perhaps the most innovative coaster-car design to date is called a fourth-dimension coaster. In this design, passenger seats are extended to either side of where the car attaches to the overhead track, and each seat of a car operates independently of the others. The track pulls the cars into loops and twists, but each seat simultaneously rotates, creating a ride that both swoops and swivels in unexpected ways.

Deciding whether riders will sit, stand, lie down, dangle from overhead rails, or spin independently in swiveling seats is an important first decision in designing a new coaster. The design of the cars will determine many other things about the ride, such as how the cars will respond and behave on the various elements of the track itself—the rises, dips, turns, loops, and twists that will make the riding experience fun.

Engineering the Track

Knowledge of the principles of physics is extremely important in the design of a roller coaster track. Rides that do not include hair-raising drops and wild turns and twists would be considered boring by today's thrill seekers. When designers include such elements in a ride, however, they must correctly predict how physical principles will make the cars and their passengers move. A sharp turn that will be executed at high speed, for example, cannot take place on a completely flat section of track. Roller coaster cars (and the passengers they are carrying) are moving objects that have inertia and will naturally continue going forward in a straight line unless some force works to change their direction. The track of a roller coaster ride acts as that force, but if it turns too sharply, the cars and their riders will be too harshly yanked in the new direction. Riders will feel as if they are being flung hard toward the outside of the curve, because their moving bodies are still striving to stay on a straight course. A track with a

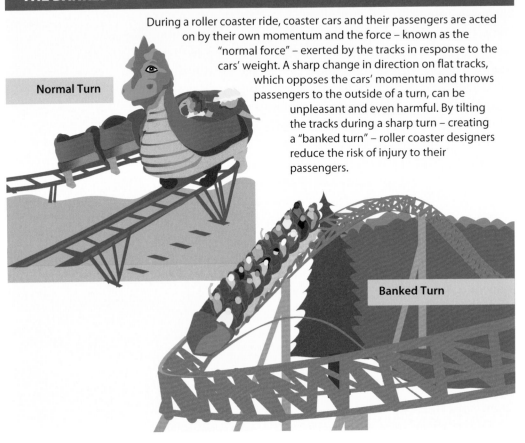

During a roller coaster ride, coaster cars and their passengers are acted on by their own momentum and the force – known as the "normal force" – exerted by the tracks in response to the cars' weight. A sharp change in direction on flat tracks, which opposes the cars' momentum and throws passengers to the outside of a turn, can be unpleasant and even harmful. By tilting the tracks during a sharp turn – creating a "banked turn" – roller coaster designers reduce the risk of injury to their passengers.

Normal Turn

Banked Turn

tight curve taken at high speed on a flat track could potentially injure passengers.

Roller coaster designers fix this problem by banking turns; they tilt the track at an angle that goes in a complementary direction to the curve. "A track pushes on the car perpendicular to the track surface," says physicist Diandra Leslie-Pelecky. "On a flat track, the push is straight up and exactly offset by the car's weight pushing down," she explains. "A banked track also pushes perpendicular to the surface, but because the surface is tilted, only part of the force pushes straight up. The rest of the force pushes toward the center of the turn."[18] On a properly banked turn, then, centripetal force pushes riders downward into their padded seats instead of yanking them roughly toward the outside of the car. Banked turns ensure a safer, smoother, and more enjoyable ride. To properly bank the turns in a coaster, however, designers must be able to calculate the speed at which cars will enter the turns, as well as the momentum they will have based on that speed due to the estimated weight of the cars when full of passengers. Designers use their knowledge of physics to determine these values and decide just the right dimensions and degree of banking that will give the coaster's every turn, loop, and flip the right mix of thrill and safety.

Blueprints: Roller Coaster Roadmaps

Roller coaster designers first decide on the type of track and car the coaster will have, choose the thrill elements such as dips, bends, and loops it will include, and calculate how turns should be banked. Then they must get their ideas down on paper. They do this in the form of a building plan called a blueprint, which is a way to communicate the exact size and dimensions of every physical component of the ride to those constructing it.

The details about a coaster must be mapped out precisely ahead of time, because roller coaster designers are not the people who actually *build* the coaster. This task falls to contractors, construction specialists who can look at a blueprint and translate it into an actual, physical ride. "Blueprints provide a universal language by which all information about a part is furnished to the craftperson," says blueprint draftsman Thomas Olivo. "An accurate mental picture can be formed from the information presented."[19] Blueprints are a vital way to communicate the designer's ideas and engineering knowledge to the construction specialists who will actually put the coaster's pieces together.

From the Ground Up

Before any coaster can be built, a construction company needs a good place to build it. An important part of a coaster's blueprint design includes its overall dimensions. Coasters take up a lot of space horizontally on the ground,

Engineers designing a roller coaster track will title the track at an angle to avoid creating turns that are too abrupt. This creates a safer and smoother ride.

but they can also require a lot of space overhead for their tallest loops and hills. Long before construction ever begins, designers carefully consider where the coaster will eventually stand. Potential barriers to its construction include not only natural ones such as hills, canyons, and vegetation but also human-made structures like roads, buildings, power lines, and even other roller coasters. In some theme parks, different rides are so close to each other that their tracks wind in and out between one another in places. All of these factors contribute to a roller coaster's final design.

Once the designer has created a building plan that will work within the physical boundaries of the coaster, builders move

Becoming a Roller Coaster Contractor

Job Description: A general contractor is a professional who guides construction projects from site preparation to finished product. Roller coaster contractors specialize in this type of construction and work closely with designers, engineers, and amusement park officials to oversee the building of a roller coaster. The general contractor is responsible for reading blueprints and design plans, hiring the necessary work crews and subcontractors (specialists in a certain type of construction, such as electrical wiring), ordering materials, and coordinating all the steps of the construction process.

Education: Most general contractors gain practical experience through a three- to five-year apprenticeship in the construction field they wish to specialize in. An undergraduate degree in business or construction management is also helpful.

Qualifications: Most states require contractors to have a license, obtained by taking courses and passing an exam. Contractors need expertise in business and management as well as construction practices. They must also be organized and skilled at making complicated decisions.

Additional Information: Contractors often own their own businesses but must be willing to travel to find projects in different areas.

Salary: $55,000 a year and up.

---

in and begin preparing the ground where the coaster will sit. "The first step in actual construction is to prepare the site," says contractor and construction educator Mark Huth. Usually, the ground needs to be level, so the first step in preparing the site is to grade it, or create the desired contours, by excavating soil from high spots or filling in any low spots to create an even starting point for the coaster. "The builder must be concerned with not only the grade or contour of the existing site," Huth says, "but also that of the finished site."[20] In other words, the way the finished coaster will be positioned on the site must also be taken into account; some coaster designs may purposely be built into hillsides, for example, to create added visual drama.

Once the site that will host the ride has been graded, a coaster needs a solid foundation. Coasters, in their final form, are massive structures that must support a lot of weight. It is essential that they are stable and structurally sound, because riders could be hurt or even killed if a coaster were to move unexpectedly or come apart. All coasters are rooted deeply into the ground at many foundation points by a method that has remained basically unchanged throughout coaster history: a deep hole is dug and then filled with concrete. If the ground surface that will hold the roller coaster is soft or sandy, large wooden posts are driven deep into the ground around the hole for each concrete foundation point. These posts anchor the concrete and ensure that the coaster's all-important foundation will not sink or move over time. Modern coaster designs might have up to two thousand concrete foundation points, making their tracks extremely sturdy and secure.

The Nuts and Bolts of Building a Coaster

A heavy metal plate is inserted in each foundation point before the concrete dries and these connector plates are later used to solidly anchor the next step of the construction process: the coaster's main supports. Clearing the ground and crafting the many concrete foundation points is critical to a coaster's construction, but the addition of the main supports is where the project begins to take the shape of a coaster. These are giant posts of wood or steel that will bear most of the track's weight once the coaster is complete. A large crane lifts the massive main support pieces into place so they can be attached to the connector plates in the concrete foundation points. Often, the main supports are held upright by temporary supportive braces until the next step of track construction. This step is the assembly of the cross braces, the smaller support pieces that straddle the gaps between the coaster's main supports to create a trestle-style structure that will ultimately support the base of the coaster track.

The construction of the main supports and cross braces is where wooden coasters usually differ from steel ones.

BITS & BYTES

47 square miles (122 sq. km)

Area encompassed by Walt Disney World in Florida, the world's largest theme park

Most wooden coasters look like small mountains built out of a meshwork of wooden supports and crosspieces. These pieces are joined together individually, using bolts and nails. Steel plates are added to reinforce important, weight-bearing joints in the structure. The entire ride is usually constructed on-site using stacks of delivered lumber. Construction workers measure and cut all the pieces individually, then use cranes to lift the pieces into place. Wooden braces prop up various parts of the design of a wooden coaster until the supporting pieces can be fastened together.

Separate sections of roller coaster track will be joined together to complete a ride in Munich, Germany. Giant posts will hold the majority of the track's weight.

Steel coasters are made differently. Their main supports, as well as the cross-pieces and the curved steel portions of track, are manufactured in factories, then brought by truck to the coaster's location. The coaster is assembled on-site, section by section, as the huge pieces are bolted and welded together. It often seems to observers that steel coasters are built more quickly than wooden ones. But spectators do not witness all the work that takes place at a factory before actual on-site construction; steel coasters just seem to spring up quickly once the large pieces are delivered. The construction process of a wooden coaster, on the other hand, plugs along piece by piece; however, the construction of any coaster is a hefty undertaking that requires many tons of material and a large cast of people to make it happen. "Believe it or not, with all the safety requirements, building a roller coaster is a lot more difficult than erecting a skyscraper,"[21] says roller coaster designer Ben Schwegler. Roller coasters are a testament to people's unique ability to take an abstract idea and transform it into a ride that is massive, complicated, and most of all, fun yet safe.

Laying the Track

Most of the construction on a roller coaster happens beneath the track itself. A solid foundation and a sturdy network of crosspieces are the most important elements in the entire design, because without them, the coaster would collapse. Yet the part of the construction process that riders care most about is the part they will actually be coasting on—the track. This is one of the last steps in the construction of a new coaster.

All coasters, even wooden ones, have steel tracks. What officially differentiates a wooden coaster from a steel one is whether the steel tracks are bolted to a wooden track foundation or a steel one. "Many wood-track coasters have a steel support structure," says Scott Rutherford. "By the same token, a few steel coasters have wood support structurework beneath those tubular steel rails. But in essence, if the track is made of laminated wood on which steel strap rails are mounted, it's a wood coaster,"[22] he explains. To make this laminated wood, several layers of flat lumber are glued together in sections. These sections are then laid in pairs, parallel to one another, and attached one by one to the massive structure that has been built for the sole purpose of shaping and

supporting the final coaster track. When the track's wooden underlayer has been laid, sections of steel track are then bolted to the wood in parallel rows. The sections of track, with the regular seams created every time two track pieces meet end-to-end, give the final ride the signature thump-thump sound and the bumpy feel of a wooden roller coaster.

Steel coasters, even if they are supported partially or completely by a wooden structure underneath, differ from the wooden variety because their tracks are made of steel tubes, formed in sections at a factory before being transported to the coaster site and attached to the substructure. The sections of preformed track are lifted by crane and put end to end, then attached to the track-support structure with bolts. Sections of track might also be welded to the track supports and to their adjoining sections, a process of adhering metal surfaces together using melted metal that forms a strong bond after it cools. Building a steel coaster with prefabricated parts is like completing a huge jigsaw puzzle. Positioning each premade section of steel track to fit perfectly with the previous section often requires additional scaffolding, or a temporary structure that holds the track's pieces in proper position until workers can attach them to each other and the support beams. Because the tracks of a steel coaster are not attached to stacks of wooden segments laid end to end, the ride's trains are able to follow curving, looping, twisting paths not possible with a wooden coaster's underlayment of planks. Steel coasters ride more smoothly and also look far different than their wooden cousins once all the support scaffolding used in their construction has been removed. Observers might never guess how similar the foundations and structural principles of both kinds of coasters really are.

The End of the Track

Construction crews, often consisting of thousands of workers, follow blueprints to erect new coaster rides bolt by bolt and piece by piece. While the track and its massive support structure are being raised, the coaster's cars are simultaneously being designed off-site at a factory. By the time the cars arrive at the track and before they take their first test run on the ride, two additional and critical elements must first be in place and working: the means for getting the cars up the first lift hill and the means for bringing them to a successful stop at the end of the ride.

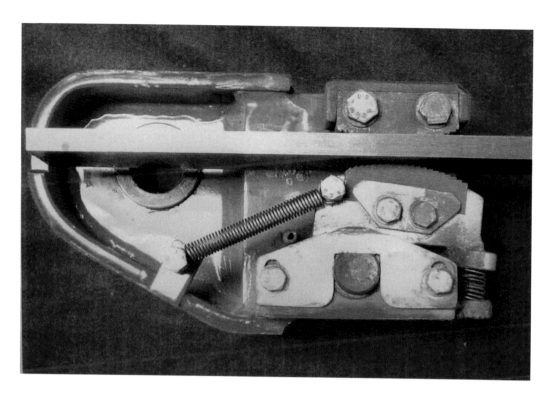

Brake mechanisms are perhaps even more important to the success of a finished roller coaster than the mechanisms that will put them in motion in the first place. Inertia, in theory, could keep a coaster in perpetual motion around the track, but every coaster ride must come to an end. Newton's laws of motion state that objects in motion will remain that way until forces act on them to bring them to a stop. Ironically, gravity—the same force that gets coasters going and keeps them moving—can also help slow a coaster down. Designers often include a portion of track that goes uphill near the end of the ride so that gravity pulls against the cars, helping to slow them down. If they were to continue going uphill long enough, the force of gravity would eventually stop their momentum without the use of any other braking method. But that would take more space than most designers can afford to incorporate into a roller coaster design.

Instead, most modern roller coasters are equipped with mechanical brakes that use friction. Just as roller coaster cars do not have onboard motors to make them go, they also

Brake mechanisms like this one help roller coasters come to a safe stop at the end of the ride. There are several different kinds of brakes, including skid brakes and fin brakes.

do not have onboard brakes to make them stop. A coaster's braking systems are instead built right into the track in the form of devices that create friction against the moving cars. Some coaster designs, usually old ones, accomplish this by adding long strips of material between the track rails near the end of the ride. Whenever a train of cars reaches that portion of the track, the material rubs against the underside of the coaster cars, creating friction that works to slow the whole train down. These are called skid brakes because the extra material on the track skids against the undersides of the cars to bring them to a halt.

Skid brakes are better than no brakes, but they have disadvantages. Depending on the size and number of riders in a train of coaster cars, the train's momentum (its mass multiplied by its velocity) can vary greatly from one load of passengers to the next. Skid brakes slow all cars the same way, making for sudden, harsh, and bumpy stopping experiences that can even injure passengers. One possible neck injury associated with skid brakes is called whiplash, which occurs when a rider is jolted to a sudden halt. "The head lags behind this motion due to its inertia," explains orthopedic specialist Jürgen Krämer. "The neck is relatively too weak to transmit these strong forces and its supporting structures are overextended." This can happen, Krämer says, in "roller coaster rides whose attraction lies in unexpected acceleration and deceleration movements."[23] The risk of whiplash injuries due to skid brakes forced engineers to seek better, smoother braking mechanisms for roller coasters.

Fast Ways to Slow Down

Another type of braking mechanism, called a fin brake, was considered a vast improvement over skid brakes and is the most common braking system in modern roller coasters. In this type of brake, an extension called a fin extends from the bottom of a roller coaster's cars. Controlled squeezing mechanisms installed in the track apply pressure (and thus, friction) to this fin whenever it is necessary to slow down or stop the train. Common squeezing mechanisms are hydraulic, using fluid pressure to press mechanical squeezing surfaces

against the fin under a car, or pneumatic, using air pressure to accomplish the same purpose. These braking mechanisms are responsible for the sharp hissing noise passengers often hear at the end of a ride when their train of cars comes to a stop.

Fin brakes have many advantages over skid brakes. For one thing, the amount of pressure exerted on the cars' fins can be modified according to the cars' momentum and how quickly the car needs to stop. Controlling the force of braking can make the stopping experience more comfortable for passengers and can prevent injuries such as whiplash. Like skid brakes, fin brakes also continue to work in the event of a power outage, ensuring that coaster cars can always be safely stopped. Fin brakes do have disadvantages, though. They are usually controlled by ride operators who engage the brakes when cars reach a certain point near the end of the track. A ride operator who is not paying attention might forget to stop the cars. This has caused accidents in which a train at the end of a ride crashes into the one in front of it. Manually controlled fin brakes are only as reliable as their human operators.

The Cheetah Hunt roller coaster at Busch Gardens in Florida uses magnets in its design to both propel cars forward and slow them to a safe stop. Magnetic brakes have become popular to include in new roller coaster designs.

Inside a Hydraulic Brake

Hydraulic brake systems are made up of connected cylinders or containers filled with a fluid (usually oil). The main cylinder, called the master cylinder, has a piston—a disc-shaped piece of metal or other material that fits tightly inside the cylinder. If the piston is pushed down, it forces the fluid in the master cylinder into the connected cylinders (called slave cylinders). The harder the master piston pushes, the more pressure the oil will exert on the outer surfaces of the connected slave cylinders.

In a hydraulic braking system, the pistons in the slave cylinders are attached to surfaces designed to grip the wheels of a coaster car and put pressure on its wheels. This pressure causes friction, a force created whenever the surface of one object slides past the surface of another. Greater pressure on the pistons creates greater friction against the wheels, which can slow or even stop the coaster car. Hydraulic brakes installed in roller coaster tracks make it possible to control the speed of the cars. Pressure just has to be exerted on the piston of the brake's master cylinder.

The master cylinder is a key component of hydraulic brakes, which are used in roller coaster tracks to control the speed of the cars.

A third kind of braking mechanism uses magnets to slow cars down. Magnets embedded at certain points of the track have an electrical charge opposite that of a magnetized metallic strip embedded in the base of each car. As the car's magnetic strip passes over the oppositely charged magnets in the track, the pull created by the attraction between the magnets creates an electrical drag force that pulls against the forward motion of the car. Magnetic brakes can effectively and smoothly slow a train of cars regardless of how full it is or how fast it is going. They also provide a silent braking experience because there are no mechanical parts that have to be engaged. These brakes cut down on maintenance costs, too, because magnetic brakes do not work by friction and therefore do not wear out or require frequent replacement.

Another advantage of magnetic brakes is that they work automatically and do not rely on human operators to engage them. "The great feature of these brakes is that they're zero maintenance, and they're beautifully foolproof,"[24] says Richard Henry, former director of operations at Kennywood Park in Pennsylvania. Magnetic brakes are an increasingly popular choice for new roller coaster designs. These, or any other brake mechanisms used in a ride, are one of the final features added to the finished coaster, because the rest of the track must be in place first. Not until a well-designed and properly functioning brake system is installed can a roller coaster be considered complete.

Ready to Ride

The process of designing and building a new amusement park ride is a long one. Crafting a track that will be both safe and exciting requires a close relationship and excellent communication between the engineers who design the ride and the contractors who actually build it. For any coaster to be a success, it must work smoothly and perfectly, so the cars are loaded with sandbags or dummies to simulate human weight, and the ride is tested repeatedly before any human passengers ever set foot on board. After that, the only thing standing between a ride and its success is people's desire and willingness to ride it. Coasters are given exciting names. Their cars are often designed after a theme. The tracks themselves are painted in attention-grabbing colors. Then, all the designers and builders can do is wait for crowds to take notice. After all, a roller coaster's popularity has always been based on human psychology and what people find to be fun.

CHAPTER 4

Experiencing the Coaster: What Makes Riding Fun

Roller coaster designers and engineers are always seeking new ways to make rides exciting, different, and even scarier than any coaster ever built before. Many roller coasters are as much architectural marvels as they are rides, rising many stories into the air as they loop and twist, their tracks sometimes even intertwining with those of other coasters. A roller coaster's physical track and design, however, only make up half of its success story. The other half comes from the people who will ride it. Roller coasters are not just made to be looked at. They are built to be ridden. The human body itself is a basic part of roller coaster success. Designing and constructing a coaster, therefore, requires not only an excellent understanding of physics and how the cars will move around the track but an equal understanding of how people's bodies and perceptions will respond to various elements of the coaster. The world's best coasters are designed to confuse (and often to terrify) their passengers. "You have to be just a little bit mean to design roller coasters,"[25] says Bill Cobb, designer of many famous wooden rides in the 1970s and 1980s, including Cyclone at Six Flags New England and Screamin' Eagle at Six Flags

St. Louis. Roller coasters would not be the incredibly popular attractions they are today if they did not have trains full of screaming riders.

Greed for Speed

Few people want to ride a roller coaster that takes a leisurely course along its track. One of the exciting things about thrill rides is their speed. The newest generation of coasters offers rides that seem to fly along the track, some reaching speeds of almost 150 miles per hour (240kph). Merely going fast is not what makes a ride fun and exciting, however. Airplanes travel more than three times that fast, averaging about 500 miles per hour (800kph), yet many riders are lulled to sleep during flight. What makes a roller coaster thrilling is its ability to give riders the perception that they are moving very fast.

People on a roller coaster may close their eyes in the excitement of the ride, but they will still be very aware of what they are not seeing. The velocity of the ride will thrill them even if they cannot see what is happening.

Upgrade: Urethane Wheels

Early roller coasters had steel wheels that were under-mounted on the track to keep the attached coaster cars firmly in place. These wheels were durable and safe, but they had disadvantages. Friction, a force created when the metal wheels rolled against the metal track, slowed cars down. Metal wheels also made early coasters incredibly noisy. The steel wheels did a poor job of absorbing shock, too. They led to very jerky and bumpy rides for passengers. Many of these problems were eliminated by the 1960s, once urethane coatings were added to roller coaster wheels. Urethane, a synthetic substance similar to rubber or plastic, can be poured, brushed, or sprayed onto a surface such as a roller coaster wheel. When it hardens, it provides a smooth, shock-absorbing buffer between the wheel and the track. Urethane is very durable, resisting scratches and tears so that coaster wheels need less maintenance. It is also inexpensive. Best of all, new kinds of urethane reduce friction between wheels and a coaster track, making it possible for coasters to zip around the tracks much faster and more smoothly than ever before.

People are most aware of their own velocity, or the speed at which they are moving in a certain direction, when they see stationary objects flying past them or at moments when they are accelerating quickly enough to feel the change in velocity. One reason airplanes seem to be traveling slowly once they are above the ground is the lack of anything stationary appearing to fly past the windows. "The visual perception of movement is based on change of position relative to other objects," says psychologist Spencer Rathus. "One way is to look for objects that you know are stable, such as platform columns, houses, signs, or trees."[26] Roller coasters whose thrills come from high speeds usually send riders close to points of reference—things on the ground that are not moving. A rider's brain instantly estimates the rate at which such stable objects seem to be flying past, then uses this information to calculate its own relative speed. When nearby trees or signs become a visual blur, it signals to the brain that the body is traveling very fast. Even though some coasters travel at speeds less than what an average car might reach on a freeway, designers often foster the illusion of great speed by sending their tracks on paths low to the ground and adding landscaping or other visible features that will appear to be flying past.

If a roller coaster rider were to close his eyes in terror throughout the entire ride, however, he would still be aware that he was traveling quickly. Human senses also gauge speed by reacting physically to acceleration, or an increase in the body's velocity. Cues that the body is accelerating rapidly are sensations such as being pushed back into the roller coaster's seat or feeling a sudden rush of air against the face. Roller coaster rides can push trains forward along the track with intense acceleration. The body's senses immediately respond to the rapid change from sitting still on the track (having no velocity) to surging forward. "Thrill rides are machines particularly designed to compel our human bodies to change state repeatedly," says mechanical engineer Ansel Urgal. "At an increased forward speed, the body is pulled back into the seat."[27]

Closing one's eyes, therefore, will not mask a person's awareness of a thrilling change in her own velocity, because it will not disguise the sensations of being pushed backward or of air rushing past her face. Some indoor rides erase visibility by plunging riders into total darkness, but they can still create the illusion of great speed, such as using wall-mounted fans to blow gusts of air into riders' faces during the ride. Whether in full daylight or total darkness, the sensations of accelerating quickly and moving at a very fast pace are two major draws of the roller coaster experience.

Falling for Roller Coasters

Roller coaster rides thrive on creating sensations that make most people uneasy. Moving forward at great speed is thrilling because the human body has a built-in wariness of crashing into something when going too fast. People are also born

A sharp, vertical drop like the Oblivion ride at an amusement park in the United Kingdom allows riders to feel like they are falling. After a brief feeling of weightlessness, called air time, riders will experience the pull of gravity as they are yanked down toward the ground.

with instincts that make them aware of how far they are above the ground, since falling could be as disastrous to one's safety as crashing. Most roller coaster designs exploit this human distrust of high places. The lift hill often serves a dual purpose: it gets the trains to a high point so that gravity will pull them down and build momentum for the rest of the ride, but it also creates uneasiness for passengers. Many lift hills give riders plenty of time to look over the side and see how far they are above the ground. The brain, meanwhile, processes the information the eyes are perceiving. The brain realizes, for example, that the smaller the appearance of things like people and vehicles, the farther away they are, so the higher the person has climbed. At the top of a lift hill, most people have a natural reaction to being so far up in the air that things below them look small. They start to produce adrenaline.

BITS & BYTES
500,000
Approximate number of people employed by U.S. amusement parks each year

Adrenaline is a hormone, a special kind of chemical produced in body organs called glands. When released into the bloodstream, hormones move around the body to make other cells and organs behave in a specific way. Adrenaline is produced in the body's two adrenal glands, one on top of each kidney. Its purpose is to help the body cope with stressful or dangerous situations. When adrenaline is released into the body, it elevates the heart rate, causes muscles to tense, and makes the senses more alert. Adrenaline basically boosts the body's excitement level. When riders are poised at the top of a roller coaster's lift hill, about to take the plunge into a fast and exhilarating ride, adrenaline flows freely through their veins and makes them feel giddy. Roller coasters that offer height as the main thrill sometimes let riders perch at the top of the hill for several seconds to contemplate being dropped. All the while, riders' hearts pump adrenaline through their veins.

Inevitably, once a coaster reaches the top of the lift hill, it does drop. The train of cars plummets down a slope that can be nearly vertical, or in some cases, so steep that it actually goes *beyond* vertical. When riders descend the back side of the lift hill on a ride called Fahrenheit at Pennsylvania's Hersheypark, for example, the track goes down at an angle of 97 degrees. The descending side of the lift hill is more than straight down, actually flexing slightly toward the ascending side. "When you come over the apex of the curve, you're lifted forward into the harness," says Kent Bachmann, director of design and engineering at Hersheypark. "The track actually disappears for a few seconds."[28]

Going down such a steep incline creates the unique sensation of falling, which is a thrill like no other. At the top of the lift hill, the body's height above the ground is stable. Once the train crests the hill and starts down the other side, however, the body begins a rapid acceleration toward the ground. As gravity pulls on the body, it creates a sinking feeling in the pit of the stomach. The body's internal organs, which were stationary at the top of the hill, shift upward slightly in the body cavity as the rest of the body momentarily drops out from underneath them.

The feeling of momentary stillness before gravity yanks one toward the earth also creates a brief sensation of weightlessness. Coaster enthusiasts and designers have a special name for it—they call it air time, because the body lifts slightly out of the coaster's seat and hangs in the air before a sudden drop. Coaster designers try to incorporate several instances of air time in every ride. Enthusiastic passengers love the flip-flop feeling they get in the pit of their stomach with sudden shifts in gravity.

Expect the Unexpected

Speed and air time are two main roller coaster features that appeal to their fans. The faster and higher a coaster goes, the more quickly it earns fame as a thrill ride. The nervous anticipation of a high drop or the singular rush of rapid acceleration are not the only things that make roller coasters fun, however. Designers also play with rider's expectations. Because people live in a world with natural laws of physics, their brains expect certain movements and experiences to have certain effects. If the body is moving forward in one direction, for example, the brain naturally expects it to continue on the same forward course, because that is what the laws of motion and inertia have trained the brain to anticipate. As the eyes look forward and process information about what is coming next, the brain sends signals to the body telling it to brace itself in preparation of what is about to happen.

Roller coaster designers deliberately try to fool the eyes and the brain by sending the track into unexpected

movements. If the senses perceive that the car is likely to turn to the right, for example, a sudden shift to the left will throw the brain into confusion and make the body feel off balance. Coaster features like inversions (upside-down loops) excel in creating this sort of confusion. A track that takes a rider into a basic overhead loop is predictable—as the rider looks forward at what is coming next, his brain processes information and he braces to rise up, turn over, and then come back down. Modern steel coasters, however, can invert riders in ways passengers cannot predict, involving features like cobra loops that take the shape of a striking cobra's hooded head, bringing riders into one overhead inversion before twisting in midair and taking them the other direction. Track features like these make it impossible for the brain to correctly process information about what is coming up. Riders plummet down the roller coaster track completely unprepared for where they will be going next.

Roller coasters with cobra loops send riders into an inversion and then twist them in midair to take them in another direction. The movements make it impossible for riders to anticipate what will happen next.

Putting on the Brakes

Roller coasters have mechanisms built into the track to stop cars at the end of a ride. Tracks are also equipped with brakes at several other portions of the ride. The track is broken down into design sections, each of which is known as a block. Every block has its own braking mechanism that can be used to slow or completely stop a train of cars. If something goes wrong with a train or the track, ride operators can use block brakes to halt cars in a safe place while the problem is being fixed. Block brakes are also important because some coasters have two or more trains of cars and may start a second train up the lift hill before the first one has completed its course. If two trains are on the track at once and there is a problem with the first one, block brakes prevent the second train from crashing into it. Modern block brakes are designed to work properly even in the event of a power outage, so roller coaster cars can be stopped whenever necessary. Block brakes are one of the things that make roller coasters safe for riders.

Even rides that do not set records for height or speed receive high praise from coaster enthusiasts as long as the track is filled with surprises that keep them on the edge of their seats—sometimes literally. The Texas Giant at Six Flags over Texas in Arlington, for example, earned 2011's Golden Ticket Award for the world's best ride, the most prestigious designation a coaster can receive. This wooden coaster is not the world's tallest or fastest ride. Its claim to fame is instead the way it confuses people's perceptions with steep drops and turns that bank unpredictably, giving passengers what they all want most in a coaster—a ride that is full of physical and psychological surprises from start to finish.

Perpetually Imbalanced

The diving, twisting, looping, and dipping action of roller coasters is calculated to confuse the brain about where it and the body are in relation to other objects. The brain has

different mechanisms for processing information about where the body is located and how it is positioned. It takes in visual information from the eyes which helps alert the brain as to whether the ground or the horizon are tilted or whether surrounding objects have turned upside down—indicating that the body is on its side or upside down. The brain also uses sensory information from the inner ears to figure out the body's exact position. Fluid contained in tubes deep inside the ear give information about the body's position above flat ground—whether it is upright, lying flat, or even flipped upside-down.

Such details tell the brain whether the body is standing or sitting upright. If the brain perceives that the body is not in a desirable position, it can send signals to the muscles to correct their position. If people did not have these constant sensory balance checks, they would not be able to stand on their feet or walk in a straight line. Usually, when a person is standing or sitting, her brain is controlling her body's movements. If she walks or runs, her brain tells her muscles to do

The up, down, around, twisting, and looping movements of a roller coaster ride can be disorienting and cause motion sickness in some riders. The brain may send signals to the body in an attempt to correct the imbalances, which of course the body cannot do as the ride continues.

Sick of Spinning

Motion sickness afflicts about one in every three people and can make riding roller coasters a miserable experience. It brings on many unpleasant symptoms. The affected person may begin to salivate, sweat, turn pale in the face, feel drowsy, get a headache, and generally feel dizzy and unwell. These symptoms can last for hours after the activity that caused them is over. Motion sickness usually leads to nausea and sometimes to vomiting. Many riders' amusement park fun has been ruined by motion sickness.

Fortunately, most sufferers can take medication to keep their symptoms in check long enough to experience the thrill of a few rides. These medications usually act on the brain by targeting neurotransmitters, chemical messengers that transmit signals from the brain to the body's cells and make them act a certain way. When experiencing motion sickness, an individual's neurotransmitters stimulate the vomiting center in the brain stem, which in turn begins the gagging reflex that leads to vomiting. Medications that stop neurotransmitters from responding this way to motion can help prevent unwelcome symptoms.

it, and the brain will automatically expect visual changes as well as shifts in the fluid of the inner ear. It will quickly compensate for these additional movements to keep the body balanced.

If a person is standing or riding on a moving object instead of planning movements herself, however, motion can confuse the brain, because the brain is not making the person move—the moving surface is. If the eyes perceive motion even when the body is sitting still in a roller coaster seat, for instance, a person may feel unbalanced. Similarly, if fluid in the inner ear shifts in a way the brain does not anticipate or expect, a feeling of being dizzy or off-balance can result. These sensations make many people feel physically ill, a phenomenon known as motion sickness. "The symptoms of motion sickness appear when the central nervous system receives conflicting messages," says Jay Marks, a physician. "Your brain receives messages that do not coordinate with each other."[29]

Roller coasters deliberately create a mismatch of the usual cues that alert the brain to movement and balance. For some people, this makes for an exhilarating ride full of surprises, but the same phenomenon can have harsh effects on others. "Motion sickness relates to our sense of balance and equilibrium," Marks says. "Researchers in space and aeronautical medicine call this sense spatial orientation, because it tells the brain where the body is 'in space': what direction it is pointing, what direction it is moving, and if it is turning or standing still."[30] A brain that is confused about its whereabouts sometimes forces the body to respond in unwelcome ways. The brain will register vertigo, a sensation of being in motion or spinning even if the body is standing still. Feelings of vertigo often lead to nausea, commonly referred to as feeling sick to one's stomach (though the phenomenon is caused entirely by the brain). Vertigo and related nausea can in turn cause physical reactions in the body. "The sudden shifting of our body's position upsets the fluid in our inner ears . . . and initiates responses like an increased heart rate and tightening in our stomach muscles,"[31] says Urgal. These feelings may even cause the brain to instigate vomiting—a reflex that causes the stomach to forcefully eject its contents. Not everyone, therefore, loves a wild roller coaster ride. The same physical feelings that create a state of euphoria in some riders make other riders throw up. People who often get motion sickness tend to look at roller coasters with dread rather than excitement.

The Fear Factor

People may be unwilling to ride roller coasters for other reasons, too. An estimated 5 percent of the world's population suffers from acrophobia, an extreme terror of high places. Staring up at some of the towering rides that exist today can scare these height-fearing park visitors away from roller coasters. Of course, most people—with or without

Not everyone loves to ride roller coasters. Those who get motion sickness from the rides might prefer to stay away, and people who are afraid of heights will be turned off by coasters' tall hills and steep drops.

acrophobia—will feel at least a little uneasy as they ascend the lift hill of a mammoth ride like the Millennium Force at Cedar Point in Sandusky, Ohio. Fear is a natural human response to being hoisted 310 feet (94m) into the air. But for people with a true phobia of heights, the experience is likely to set off a full-blown panic attack that can raise their heart rate, make them hyperventilate (breathe faster or more deeply than normal), cause them to shake uncontrollably, and even give them chest pain. A person with a phobia may feel extreme anxiety, or panic, even in a situation that poses no true danger. "Anxiety has psychological and physical features," says Rathus. "Psychological features include worrying, fear of the worst things happening, losing control, nervousness, and inability to relax. Physical features . . . include trembling, sweating, a pounding or racing heart, elevated blood pressure (a flushed face), and faintness."[32]

With or without acrophobia, most people's brains naturally activate an anxiety response at the top of a roller coaster's lift hill. Even though they may be strapped into the cars by safety harnesses and may trust the overall safety of the ride, being so high off the ground usually engages the body's stress response. There is always some degree of worry, for example, that one could fall off the ride. Even people who do not have a true phobia of heights feel anxious at the top of a lift hill, especially a record-breaking one like the Kingda Ka, which takes riders to the elevation of a forty-five-story structure. "You feel like . . . you're going to die," says Kirun Mir, commenting on the experience of riding Kingda Ka. "At the top it feels like you're falling off a building. It was out of control."[33] Anxiety is an appropriate response to being so far off the ground. For someone with a phobia of heights, though, the dread of feeling like they might die is so great that they likely will refuse to get anywhere near a roller coaster much less ride on one. Even people who do not have a full-fledged phobia of heights usually have a certain psychological threshold when it comes to roller coasters. Some of them are simply too frightening for some would-be riders.

BITS & BYTES
3 hours
Average wait time to ride Kingda Ka, the world's tallest coaster (longer, to sit in the front row)

Safely Scary

Despite their capacity for making people throw up and for setting off panic attacks due to a sense of imminent death, roller coasters nevertheless remain a tremendously popular pursuit for people all over the world, and for many riders, the scarier the coaster, the better. Amusement parks that profit from people's penchant for craving terrifying thrills

The Fuji-Q Highland amusement park in Japan has a scary-looking roller coaster, and many people like the scares they get from the rides. No matter how scary they look, however, all coasters are designed to be safe.

deliberately make their roller coasters seem as frightening as possible by giving them names and logos that hint at danger, names like Intimidator at Carowinds in Charlotte, North Carolina; Scream! at Six Flags Magic Mountain in Valencia, California; and Takabisha, meaning "dominant," at Fuji-Q Highland in Yamanashi, Japan.

Most roller coaster names and themes are deliberately chosen to daunt visitors, sometimes even daring them to climb aboard. Yet, instead of scaring people away, these coasters tend to have the opposite effect. An unwritten amusement park rule is that the scarier a ride is touted to be, the longer the line of people who will wait to ride it. "People like to experience fear . . . as in horror movies and haunted houses," says Bill Linkenheimer, a longtime member and former president of American Coaster Enthusiasts, a club of roller coaster fans. He adds, "You know you aren't *really* putting yourself in danger, but it's a way of going out of control at crazy speeds without risking your life."[34]

Roller coaster rides, no matter how tall, fast, or twisted, are one thing above all others—safe. Though they are designed and constructed to give as wild and frightening a ride as possible, riders are willing to try them because they know that roller coasters are perhaps the most risk-free way on earth for humans to experience such incredible speeds or gut-wrenching drops. The safety record of roller coasters is an important cornerstone of the global amusement park industry and what keeps so many visitors coming back for more. While technology makes it possible to build rides that are taller, faster, and seemingly more death-defying than ever, it is also vital to reassure today's park operators and visitors that no actual harm will befall people on rides. The balance between providing ever-evolving thrills and maintaining safety determines what engineers can invent to keep the coaster industry fresh and exciting within the bounds of passenger protection.

CHAPTER 5

Coaster Technology of the Future

Roller coaster manufacturers are in the business of creating fear and terror in their riders. Today's best-known thrill rides compete with others around the world for the title of tallest, fastest, and overall scariest in a race to be named the best roller coaster on earth. Manufacturers blend their knowledge of science, technology, and what people find both psychologically and physically terrifying to create ever more innovative tracks. Roller coasters have become a very big business. According to the International Association of Amusement Parks and Attractions (IAAPA), the organization that oversees roller coaster rides and attractions in the United States and many other countries around the world, more than 300 million tickets to U.S. amusement parks are sold each year, surpassing the nation's entire population. Altogether, American park goers take 1.7 billion rides down roller coasters every year and bring in $9 billion in revenue, more than four times the amount of money Americans spend to go to the movies each year.

The popularity of roller coasters creates a continuing challenge, however. Coaster enthusiasts are always seeking something faster and scarier than anything they have experienced before. Designers and engineers, therefore, endlessly aim to satisfy the demand for innovative coaster experiences. Exciting developments are always on the horizon in this changing industry. Technological discoveries might make the impossible seem possible and could lead to future rides more terrifying than any that exist today. As rides grow taller, faster, and more complex, however, coasters may also reach limits that result from technology, concern for rider safety, and the reality of what the average human body can physically tolerate during a ride. Coaster riders may also reach a fear threshold, as they determine how scary is too scary. The industry constantly needs to stay up to date on what riders want in new coaster rides and what safety on a ride truly means.

Mega Record Breakers

Roller coasters are classified in many ways—by whether they are made of wood or steel, for example, and also by the way the cars attach to the track, such as inverted coasters and those that travel on top of the track. In the past two decades, another type of classification has emerged for coasters that break height boundaries. So-called megacoasters, also known as hypercoasters, reach a height (usually followed by a drop) of at least 200 feet (61m). The first megacoaster was the Magnum XL-200 at Cedar Point in Ohio. Built in 1989, this was the first roller coaster in the world to have such a tall lift hill. In the decade that followed, megacoasters were built around the world, each design trying to best the current record holder by a few feet. In 2000 Cedar Point came out with another record setter, the aptly named Millennium Force. Reaching 310 feet (95m) at its crest, it dwarfed the world's megacoasters and was named the first gigacoaster, a name now reserved for rides that break the 300-foot (91m) barrier. As of 2012, there are only eight gigacoasters in the world. The newest, with an opening date of May 2012, is Leviathan in Ontario, Canada.

Rider Protection

Roller coasters are a huge business, and one ticket to their success is their safety record. Despite their quest to keep terrified riders on the edges of their seats, coasters have a remarkably low rate of passenger injury. Riders are confident that although they may feel as if they are going to fall out, they will reach the end of the track in one safe, if shaky, piece. Roller coasters, today a multibillion-dollar worldwide industry, depend on achieving nearly flawless safety records, because if park visitors regularly got hurt on coasters, expensive lawsuits would follow and people would simply stop paying to ride. The industry also feels a moral responsibility to make sure that no one who climbs aboard any ride climbs off in worse physical shape (with the exception, perhaps, of feeling queasy). "While the amusement park and attractions industry is in the business of fun, the owners, operators and suppliers take all aspects of this business very seriously, especially when it comes to ride safety," says the IAAPA. "Amusement facilities are designed to safely deliver enjoyment and

A worker situates a test dummy in a roller coaster in preparation for a safety check. Amusement parks aim to make their rides as safe as possible, with multiple systems in place to keep people secure.

fun to their guests, so it is especially troubling when a guest is injured. Thus, operators and manufacturers work continuously to provide a safe and enjoyable visit for every guest."[35]

The IAAPA strictly regulates the roller coaster industry, imposing safety rules on every step of the design and construction of a new ride. It also has strict regulations that tell manufacturers how many times rides must be tested before allowing human passengers on board, as well as how often and in what ways every feature of a ride must be regularly inspected. The rules that roller coaster builders and operators must follow are numerous, strict, and continually evolving. Behind the scenes of every amusement park is a large team of workers constantly ensuring that every part of every coaster works properly and safely every time it goes around the track. According to Six Flags, the largest regional theme park company in the world, "There are dozens of redundant safety systems in place to protect the well-being of passengers, no matter what happens."[36] The company says its rides have computers that constantly monitor the condition and location of every coaster train throughout the ride, and if any sensor indicates a problem, all coaster trains are stopped at a safe place on the track while the problem is investigated. "It is through a complete universe of practices behind the scenes that parks like those of Six Flags can achieve the goal of making extraordinary thrills extraordinarily safe,"[37] the company claims.

The tight rules and regulations all roller coasters must follow have made coaster rides an extremely safe pastime. The IAAPA requires amusement parks to submit detailed reports on any accidents or injuries that happen on their coasters. Of the 1.7 billion U.S. coaster rides taken each year, only about 1,000 yearly injuries are reported, on average. Of those, only an average of 60 to 70 are serious enough to require an overnight hospital stay. According to statistics collected by the U.S. Consumer Products Safety Commission, which investigates amusement park accidents, the odds of dying on a roller coaster built on a fixed site in an amusement park in the United States are about 1 in 90 million. By comparison, the National Safety Council reports that the odds of dying in an automobile accident are about 1 in 6,500. The odds of being injured while riding a bicycle or jumping on a trampoline are hundreds of times higher than while riding a coaster, too. "In short, based on government data, over 99.99 percent of those guests who board rides at parks and attractions enjoy their experience without any incident whatsoever,"[38] says the IAAPA.

The Danger of Gravity

There are, however, rare occasions when passengers do get injured on roller coasters. Most rides have bars that clamp down on riders' laps or padded harnesses that fit over

Deadly g's

People can be exposed to gravitational force, or g-force, in different ways. It can be localized, affecting only a portion of the body, as in getting slapped on the back. It can also be momentary, or lasting only briefly, such as hard forces endured in a car crash. A third type of g-force is sustained, or lasting for at least several seconds. Sustained, body-wide g-forces are the most dangerous to people. The body usually withstands localized or momentary g-force better than sustained g-force, which can be deadly because blood is forced into the legs, depriving the rest of the body (and especially the brain) of oxygen. Sustained g-force applied while the body is horizontal, or lying down, instead of sitting or standing tends to be more tolerable to people, because blood pools in the back (if one is lying on one's back) and not the legs. Thus, blood, and life-giving oxygen, are easier for the heart to circulate to the brain. Some people, such as astronauts and fighter jet pilots, undergo special training exercises to increase their bodies' resistance to g-force. For most people, though, sustained g-forces of more than ten g's can be deadly, as can any g-force over a hundred g's, even a momentary or localized one.

People on roller coasters experience increased gravitational force on their bodies. This is the same g-force experienced by astronauts in a space shuttle during takeoff.

passengers' shoulders. These safety devices are designed to keep riders in place even when passenger cars plunge over steep hills or turn upside down in loops and twists. Most rides also have strict height and weight specifications to help ensure that safety harnesses or restraints will fit each passenger properly and lessen the risk that anyone will fall out of the ride. There have been extremely few instances of anyone actually being ejected from an amusement park roller coaster ride. Nevertheless, the rides that require the most advanced safety harnesses are precisely the ones that are most likely to cause injury, because they are usually the ones that seek to defy the rules of gravity.

The greatest danger in modern roller coasters that set records for height, speed, steepness, and sudden turns has far more to do with the gravitational forces that are placed on riders' bodies during these riding experiences than with the risk that riders will come out of their harnesses. Gravitational force, or g-force, is a measure of the force of gravity on an object or a measure of its acceleration through space. The earth's gravity pulls people down toward the planet's center at a constant force. At the earth's surface, therefore, people experience a gravitational force equal to 1 g, which is equivalent to their body weight on earth. Whenever an object accelerates, or increases the speed at which it is moving through space, its rate of acceleration can be given as a measure of g-force, or some multiple of the standard force of gravity. An increased g-force increases the pressure on a person's body in direct proportion to his or her weight. For example, if a woman who weighs 100 pounds (45.4kg) experiences an acceleration force of three g's, the force is the equivalent of putting 300 pounds (136kg) of pressure against her body.

G-forces affect a person any time she is pushed forward or backward in a straight line but also if she is traveling on a curved path. Her velocity, or rate of speed, going into a curve on the track of a roller coaster, for example, creates an acceleration force against the curving track. Her body resists the curved motion because inertia makes her body want to continue moving forward in the direction it was going. The acceleration, or change in the rate of speed over time, experienced throughout the turn is felt as a constant pressure pushing her toward the outside of the curved surface (or, if the track is banked, pushing her downward into her coaster seat). This acceleration pressure can be measured in g's. A force of three g's is experienced by the rider as feeling like she weighs three times her normal weight as her body moves through the curve. The faster she is going while heading into the curve, and also the sharper the turn she makes, the stronger the g-force that will be exerted on her body.

There are limits to how much g-force a person's body can safely withstand. A space shuttle during takeoff only exerts about three g's of force on the astronauts inside, for example, because even though the shuttle lifts off the earth's surface and accelerates quickly, it is traveling in a straight line. A racecar track with tight curves, by comparison, can put more than five g's of force on drivers, because moving through a curve adds more g-force than moving in a straight line. Racecar drivers often enter a curve at more than 200 miles per hour (322kph) and experience acceleration throughout the turn, creating significantly more powerful g-forces than a space shuttle liftoff.

Regulating G-Forces Responsibly

Roller coaster tracks, like racecar tracks, incorporate turns that are navigated at high speeds, and many rides exert substantial g-forces on riders. The severity of these forces and the duration of exposure to them during a ride are important considerations for coaster engineers. If a person experiences a large amount of g-force for an extended period of time, it can be more dangerous for the body than momentary exposure to that same force. People's bodies have veins and arteries that are filled with blood, and putting too much pressure on the circulatory system in the form of g-forces can impair the heart's ability to pump blood normally and the ability of the arteries and veins to carry it. Being exposed to too much g-force for too long can cause blood to pool low in the body, preventing it from bringing necessary oxygen to the brain. Airplane pilots who steer their planes into tight, high-speed turns, for instance, have been known to lose consciousness as a result of prolonged exposure to g-forces, affecting their circulation and limiting the oxygen that gets to their brain.

Fast-moving, fast-turning roller coasters pose a potential risk of exposing riders to dangerous g-forces, too. The result could be riders who lose consciousness on rides or even suffer burst blood vessels due to severe acceleration pressure during a ride. There have been cases of amusement park visitors who have lost their lives for this reason, leading many people—including lawmakers—to demand stricter design regulations for roller coasters. "This is a rapidly growing problem that will soar out of control if the industry does not wake up to its responsibility to the riding public," says U.S. congressman Edward Markey. "The average roller coaster riders are not graduates of astronaut training . . . and they surely should not be placed in a situation where the forces of the ride test the limits of human endurance,"[39] he warns. Average riders can safely tolerate a limit of only about three to four g's for an extended period of time on a roller coaster ride. Incorporating ever higher drops and faster turns on their new designs while also making sure riders are not exposed to unsafe g-forces during the ride is one of the steepest challenges modern coaster designers face.

Computer-assisted design (CAD) software allows roller coasters to be designed on a computer screen and in 3D. The CAD software allows for simulations and the calculation of gravitational force.

Computer-Assisted Design

Just as technology is making faster and potentially more dangerous roller coasters possible, however, technology is also allowing coaster designers to build safer rides. One of the most important advancements in roller coaster technology

in the past several decades has been computer-assisted design (CAD) software, computer programs that let designers create all aspects of a roller coaster on a computer screen. Such programs have become a vital part of building modern roller coasters. The programs are a vast improvement over the two-dimensional, paper blueprints that coaster designers typically used before the 1970s. Roller coaster designs often must be changed hundreds or even thousands of times to incorporate different elements or to fix problems, and a CAD program makes these changes fast and easy to make.

Another benefit of CAD technology is that it allows coaster designers to create three-dimensional representations of their designs and then rotate the images. Tracks can be viewed on screen from any angle, including above and below. Programs can give simulations of how the cars themselves are expected to behave on the track, too—all before the track is even built. "We can play the video animation for clients so they can see what the vehicle looks like as seen from a spot on the ground," says senior roller coaster designer Craig Breckenridge. "Or, we can show them what the ride looks like from the front seat."[40] Not only do CAD programs give coaster designers the ability to show their ideas to those who might buy their designs, they also help construction crews visualize how a ride should look before, during, and after the construction process.

Most importantly, CAD programs have become essential to creating safe roller coaster rides. A CAD program can calculate exactly how much g-force a track design will exert on riders at any given point. "We . . . run dynamic simulations that tell us the forces a passenger will experience during a ride," says Breckenridge. "When someone sits in a seat, their body can still move, much like a lever, and experience greater g forces than we would measure along the track's center line. We want to ensure a ride doesn't put too much strain on the rider."[41] Knowing these values as they create a new track allows designers to decide on a hill's slope, bank a turn

BITS & BYTES

$25 million

Cost to build Top Thrill Dragster, a rapid-acceleration coaster at Cedar Point in Ohio differently, or alter the dimensions of a loop or twist in ways that will lessen the physical forces placed on riders' bodies.

CAD programs can also improve coaster safety by helping designers calculate the maximum possible arm and leg reach of a human rider to make sure that a coaster's cars will never pass close enough to any obstacle for a passenger's limbs to strike against anything. A CAD program can even calculate how a track and its cars will behave in different weather conditions. Parts of a track with the sun beating down on them during a hot day might expand, for example, or on a cold and cloudy day, they might slightly shrink. CAD programs help designers predict where and how to build flexibility into tracks, as well as what kind of weather conditions could make a roller coaster unsafe for riding. All of these calculations and changes are made long before the ride is constructed, so designers know the finished product will be safe for human passengers.

With CAD programs, coaster designers are able to create new designs limited only by their own imaginations and the demands of safety. Roller coasters cost millions of dollars to build, but with CAD software, designers know the finished tracks will be both safe and successful even before the first concrete foundation point is poured. CAD programs are one of the most significant technological advancements in the history of the roller coaster industry, making it possible to construct modern rides that are totally unpredictable for passengers but very predictable for builders and designers whose top priority is rider safety.

Coasters with Magnetic Personalities

Modern roller coasters created with the help of computers still rely on basic concepts of gravity and potential and kinetic energy, and new technology is also finding its way into the physical designs of coasters to make them more exciting than ever before. One important advancement has been the linear induction motor (LIM), a system for launching modern coaster trains into motion. A LIM uses electromagnets, devices that use electricity to create a magnetic field. All magnets work because of electrical charges.

THE HYDRAULIC LAUNCH

In a hydraulic launch system, pressurized nitrogen gas and hydraulic fluid are stored in tanks, called accumulators. During launch, hydraulic fluid is sent to a series of motors that control a winch – a cylindrical drum with a chain or cable coiled around it. The steel cables around the winch attach to a catch car, which runs underneath the roller coaster train. When the motors turn the winch, the catch car launches the roller coaster into action.

The hydraulic launch was introduced in 2002, and there are currently 14 roller coasters that use this method of propulsion. In 2010 the hydraulic launch roller coaster Formula Rossa set a new speed record at 149 mph.

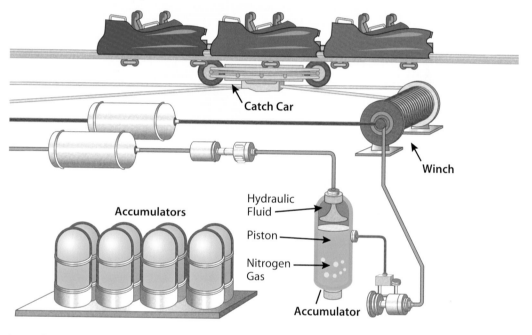

Source: Information from Brooke Borel. "How It Works: The World's Fastest Roller Coaster." PopSci. http://www.popsci.com/technology/article/2011-03/how-it-works-worlds-fastest-rollercoaster.

Atoms, the smallest particles of a substance, often have either a positive or a negative electrical charge. Atoms with opposite charges will be pulled toward one another. Metals commonly have electrically charged atoms, so one kind of metal is often strongly attracted to a certain other kind, making the two metals pull together when they come into contact with each other. In an electromagnet, a current of electricity is passed through wire coiled around a metal core. The result is a strong magnetic field, which will attract or repulse electrically charged materials. Changing the strength of the

Inside an Electromagnet

All matter is made of tiny particles called atoms. These atoms, especially in metals, often have a tiny electrical charge. If the atoms line up a certain way, their charges all point in the same direction, giving the entire piece of metal an electrical charge that can attract or repel other substances—usually metallic ones. In other words, the metal becomes magnetized. An electromagnet is a device that aligns all the atoms in a piece of metal. It is constructed by wrapping a wire of a conductive metal (such as copper) around a metal core and then attaching both ends of the wire to a battery or other source of electricity. When electricity flows through the wire, it aligns the atoms of the metal core around which it is wrapped, magnetizing the piece of metal. Increasing the strength of electricity increases the magnet's strength, up to the point where all of its atoms are aligned. Cutting off the electricity demagnetizes the device. Large, powerful electromagnets can be regulated simply by controlling the flow of electricity that runs through the wire coiled around them. Electromagnets are a very useful source of power for launching roller coasters.

electrical current changes the strength of the magnet. The pull of an electromagnet can be extremely powerful, but the magnet's strength can also be adjusted by lessening the current running through it.

Some roller coasters use the strong pull of electromagnets to build instantaneous momentum that will carry cars to the top of a lift hill. A motor creates an electrical charge to send through an electromagnet embedded in the track. Magnets on the bottom of the roller coaster's cars have an opposite charge to the electromagnet on the track. The two magnetic forces are therefore strongly attracted to one another. When current is run through the electromagnets on the track, ahead of the coaster cars, they create a tremendous pull on the magnets along the bottom of the cars, capable of launching the cars into motion. One example of a coaster that uses a

An eletromagnet constructed by wire wrapped around conductive metal that is attached to a battery can attract the atoms in metals, like the paperclips shown here. Powerful electromagnets can control the flow of electricity and be used to launch roller coasters.

LIM launch method is the Wicked Twister at Cedar Point in Sandusky, Ohio. "We're using such a massive jolt of electricity on the Wicked Twister that it would be enough to power 550 average sized houses,"[42] says Monty Jasper, the park's vice president of maintenance and new construction. When the operator of a ride with a LIM launch engages the electrical current to create the electromagnetic field, the train of cars surges forward, often reaching a speed of 60 miles per hour

(96kph) or more in less than four seconds. The technology is so powerful that the National Aeronautics and Space Administration (NASA) is even working on ways to use LIMs in space-shuttle takeoffs.

Magnetic motors are one example of how modern technology is changing the experience of riding a roller coaster, but magnetism may find its way into coasters of the future in other ways as well. Powerful magnetic fields might even be able to lift roller coaster cars off the tracks. Instead of rolling on wheels throughout a ride, cars of the future might actually hover over the metal below. This technology, called magnetic levitation, or maglev for short, could result in the world's first perfectly smooth and silent roller coaster rides. Maglev is already widely considered to be the future of high-speed train travel. Applied to roller coasters, it could change the entire riding experience, perhaps bringing about coasters that are faster, steeper, and smoother than ever before.

Another benefit of maglev technology would be a precise ability to speed cars up or slow them down at necessary places along a track, simply by adjusting the strength of the magnet's pull. Computerized sensors added all along the tracks of many coasters give constant readings of the weight, velocity, and stability of the cars themselves, as well as weather conditions like temperature and wind that could affect the safety or performance of a ride. Paired with computerized magnetic technology, rides of the future might even be able to eliminate human operators and run completely on computer readings that are constantly and instantly being calculated and checked. Not only could such coaster tracks loom higher and plunge steeper than before, injuries caused by the error of human operators could become a thing of the past.

Coasting into a New Era

The future holds few limits for roller coasters and their enthusiastic fans. As long as roller coaster designers and builders can continue to guarantee safe passage for riders, there is no end in sight for the roller coaster's ongoing journey. Coaster enthusiasts will likely always seek out a roller coaster's unique, dizzying, stomach-dropping form of thrills. At present, the industry knows no bounds. With almost twenty-five hundred roller coasters operating around the world and bringing in billions of dollars annually, the industry is alive and well. Only time will tell whether technology will ever limit coasters' ability to take people higher and faster and still bring them back to the ground safely. Perhaps the high cost of building such enormous and technically advanced machines will one day dampen new coaster developments; or perhaps, even if designers can promise that new coasters are safe, they may simply become too frightening for the average person to ride.

For now, however, roller coasters—both the new and the old—continue to take passengers up and down their tracks all over the world every day of the year. And roller coaster engineers still seem to have many tricks up their sleeves. If there are any boundaries on what roller coasters will be able to do or who will be daring enough to ride them, these limits are still far in the future.

NOTES

Chapter 1:
Thrill Rides, Then and Now

1. Spike Carlsen. *A Splintered History of Wood*. New York: HarperCollins, 2008, p. 341.
2. Carlsen. *Splintered History*, p. 342.
3. Brian Black. *Nature and the Environment in Nineteenth-Century American Life*. Westport, CT: Greenwood Press, 2006, p. 135.
4. David W. Francis and Diane DeMali Francis. *The Golden Age of Roller Coasters in Vintage Postcards*. Chicago: Arcadia, 2003, p. 7.
5. Francis and Francis. *Golden Age of Roller Coasters*, p. 7.
6. Edo McCullough. *Good Old Coney Island: A Sentimental Journey into the Past*. 1957. Reprint, Bronx, NY: Fordham University Press, 2000, p. 251.
7. Francis and Francis. *Golden Age of Roller Coasters*, p. 8.
8. Steven J. Urbanowicz. *The Roller Coaster Lover's Companion: A Thrill-Seeker's Guide to the World's Best Coasters*. New York: Kensington, 2002, p. 6.
9. Todd. H. Throgmorton. *Roller Coasters: United States and Canada.* 3rd ed. Jefferson, NC: McFarland, 2009, p. 13.

Chapter 2:
How Coasters Roll: The Physics of the Coaster Phenomenon

10. Scott Rutherford. *The American Roller Coaster*. St. Paul, MN: Motorbooks International, 2004, p. 117.
11. Richard P. McCall. *Physics of the Human Body*. Baltimore: Johns Hopkins University Press, 2010, p. 76.
12. McCall. *Physics of the Human Body*, p. 74.
13. McCall. *Physics of the Human Body*, p. 75.
14. Quoted in *National Geographic News.* "Roller Coaster Pictures: 125 Years of Thrills," October 28, 2010. http://news.nationalgeographic.com/news/2009/06/photogalleries/roller coaster-pictures-anniversary/photo2.html.
15. Rutherford. *American Roller Coaster*, p. 120.
16. Steve Miller. *The Complete Idiot's Guide to the Science of Everything*. New York: Alpha Books, 2008, p. 37.

Chapter 3:
From Blueprint to Ride: Building a Coaster

17. Quoted in Michael Yeomans. "Roller Coasters Use Magnetic Brakes." *Pittsburgh Tribune-Review*, May 1, 2005. www.pittsburghlive.com/x/pittsburghtrib/s_329728.html#ixzz1o0ebvpHB.

18. Diandra Leslie-Pelecky. *The Physics of Nascar*. New York: Dutton, 2008, p. 152.

19. Thomas P. Olivo. *Basic Blueprint Reading and Sketching*. 8th ed. Clifton Park, NY: Delmar, 2005, p. 1.

20. Mark W. Huth. *Understanding Construction Drawings*. 5th ed. Clifton Park, NY: Delmar, 2010, pp. 59–60.

21. Quoted in Matt Villano. "Mousing Around: Disney Goes for 4-D CAD in Planning Its Latest Big Park." *CIO*, June 2001, p. 146.

22. Rutherford. *American Roller Coaster*, p. 117.

23. Jürgen Krämer. *Intervertebral Disc Diseases*. 2nd ed. New York: Thieme Medical, 1990, p. 92.

24. Quoted in Yeomans. "Roller Coasters Use Magnetic Brakes."

26. Spencer A. Rathus. *Psychology: Concepts and Connections*. 9th ed. Belmont, CA: Thomson Wadsworth, 2005, p. 158.

27. Ansel C. Urgal. *Living Better: A Guide to Health, Happiness, and Managing Stress*. New York: Eloquent Books, 2009, pp. 88–89.

28. Quoted in Erin McCarthy. "Building America's Most Extreme New Roller Coaster." *Popular Mechanics*, June 10, 2008. www.popularmechanics.com/technology/engineering/extreme-machines/4268108.

29. Jay W. Marks. "Motion Sickness." MedicineNet.com. www.medicinenet.com/motion_sickness/article.htm.

30. Marks. "Motion Sickness."

31. Urgal. *Living Better*, p. 88.

32. Rathus. *Psychology*, p. 523.

33. Quoted in *New York Magazine Summer Guide*. "Scare the Hell Out of the Kids," June 26, 2005. http://nymag.com/guides/summer/12143/.

34. Quoted in *Carnegie Magazine*. "Scream Machines: The Science of Roller Coasters," January 7, 2001. www.carnegiemuseums.org/cmag/bk_issue/2000/sepoct/feat4.html.

Chapter 4:
Experiencing the Coaster: What Makes Riding Fun

25. Quoted in Austin B. Watson. "Profile: Roller Coaster Man." *Rotarian*, December 1990, p. 50.

Chapter 5:
Coaster Technology of the Future

35. International Association of Amusement Parks and Attractions. "Amusement Ride Injury Statistics," 2011. www.iaapa.org/pressroom/

AmusementRideInjuryStatistics
.asp.

36. Quoted in S. Anton Clavé. *The Global Theme Park Industry*. Cambridge, MA: CAB International, 2007, p. 426.

37. Quoted in Clavé. *Global Theme Park Industry*, p. 425.

38. Quoted in Jessica Reaves and Frank Pellegrini. "The New Roller Coasters: Thrills, Chills and Few Spills." *Time*, June 26, 2001. www.time.com/time/nation/article/0,8599,165350,00.html#ixzz1gzvLlWUR.

39. Quoted in Paul Ruben. "Scared to Death." *Popular Mechanics*, August 2003, p. 51.

40. Quoted in Jon Titus. "Engineers Take CAD Tools for a Wild Ride." *Design News*, July 8, 2010. www.designnews.com/document.asp?doc_id=229184.

41. Quoted in Titus. "Engineers Take CAD Tools for a Wild Ride."

42. Quoted in Maureen Byko. "Materials Give Roller Coaster Enthusiasts a Reason to Scream." *JOM*, May 2002. www.tms.org/pubs/journals/jom/0205/byko-0205.html.

GLOSSARY

acceleration: An increase in a moving object's velocity, or rate of motion.

adrenaline: A hormone produced in the body in response to high-stress situations.

centrifugal force: A force that makes a moving body move away from the center point of a circle.

electromagnet: A magnet created by an electrical current and whose strength can be changed by adjusting the strength of the current.

energy: The ability of one physical thing to work on or cause change in another.

friction: A retarding force created whenever two surfaces move against each other; it reduces the kinetic energy of the movement and changes it into heat energy.

g force: Gravitational force; a pressure or force exerted on an object that gives it weight relative to its size, so that a force of one g would be equal to the body's normal weight on earth.

gravity: The force that attracts a body with mass toward any other body with mass.

inertia: An object's resistance to changes in its state of motion or state of rest.

kinetic energy: The energy of an object in motion.

linear induction motor: A motor that produces movement using the attractive forces of opposing magnetic fields.

mass: A measure of the amount of matter in an object.

momentum: A measure of an object's motion, found by multiplying its mass by its velocity.

potential energy: Energy stored in a body due to its position.

velocity: The rate at which a moving object's position is changing in a given direction; in physics, it means not just speed, but speed plus direction of movement.

Books

Steven Alcorn. *Theme Park Design: Behind the Scenes with an Engineer.* Charleston, SC: CreateSpace, 2010. Examines theme parks and their rides from the perspective of a park engineer who has worked for Disney World. Explains how such parks are created, including the mechanics of popular rides and how they are controlled, as well as audiovisual details, special effects, and more.

Scott Rutherford. *The American Roller Coaster.* St. Paul, MN: Andover Junction, 2004. Covers roller coaster history from the 1880s to 2005, with descriptions of how various kinds of roller coasters are built and how they work. Written by a charter member of American Coaster Enthusiasts (ACE).

Lynne M. Stone. *Roller Coasters.* Vero Beach, FL: Rourke, 2002. Describes the history and types of roller coasters, their construction, and the physics of how they operate.

DVDs

eOne Vision. *Popular Mechanics for Kids: Rip-Roaring Roller Coasters and All Access to Fun.* DVD. Port Washington, NY: Koch Vision, 2004. Gives a history of roller coasters and illustrates the physical principles behind them, including how the created forces keep riders in their seats.

Websites

Design a Roller Coaster (www.learner .org/interactives/parkphysics/coaster) Simulation lets visitors design their own roller coaster online. Does not require knowledge of math formulas or complex physics. Explains how and why different components of a coaster will be successful.

Roller Coaster Database (www.rcdb .com) Searchable online database with statistics on almost three thousand roller coasters around the world. Find coasters based on height, length, speed, steepness, and more. Includes locations and links to information about specific coasters.

INDEX

PICTURE CREDITS

Cover photo: © 2009fotofriends/
Shutterstock.com

© 2010/Joel A. Rogers/Coaster Gallery
.com, 27

© AFP/Getty Images, 47

© Andrew Fox/Alamy, 70

© AP Images/Al Behrman, 29

© AP Images/Jay Nolan, 63

© AP Images/John Kuntz, 54

© AP Images/NJ Community Affairs
Dept, 61

© AP Images/Paul M. Walsh, 84

© Bettmann/Corbis, 8 (top right)

© Charles Taylor/ShutterStock.com, 23

© Corbis Flirt/Alamy, 78

© Everett Collection Inc/Alamy, 37

© Gale, Cengage Learning, 22, 25, 34,
42, 52, 93

© Gary Dobner/Alamy, 45, 50

© GeoStills/Alamy, 73

© Guy Shapira/ShutterStock.com, 64

© Historical Picture Archive/Corbis,
8 (top left)

© imagebroker/Alamy, 57

© Ioannis Pantzi/ShutterStock.com, 32

© Jack Picone/Alamy, 75

© Jumana El Heloueh/Reuters/Landov,
9 (top)

© Kelly-Mooney Photography/Corbis,
9 (bottom)

© Lourens Smak/Alamy, 95

© RAGMA IMAGES/ShutterStock
.com, 90

© Russell Kord/Alamy, 43

© SuperStock/Alamy, 87

© Ted Streshinsky/CORBIS, 67

© The Granger Collection, New York.
Reproduced by permission, 15, 17, 20

© Tips Images/Tips Italia Srl a socio
unico/Alamy, 11

© Toby de Silva/Alamy, 80

© ZUMA Wire Service/Alamy, 59

Jenny MacKay writes nonfiction books for kids and teens and especially likes to write books about science. She lives in northern Nevada with her husband and two children. Since there are no major amusement parks with roller coasters in northern Nevada, her family travels often to visit parks in California. Wooden roller coasters are her favorite.